ALL-TIME BEST

GREEN BAY PACKERS

TRIVIA QUIZ BOOK

Unlock the Ultimate Packers Knowledge with Fun Facts, NFL History, and Trivia Questions to Challenge Any Packer Fan at Any Age.

Joe Fletcher

Packer Fan & Trivia Pro

Thank You!

Hey Packers fans, thanks so much for purchasing this trivia book. It was a true labor of love, and I hope you enjoy it.

If you'd like to discover even more fun facts about one of the oldest teams in the NFL, the Green Bay Packers, head on over to my website, Packerland.

www.packer.land

Follow Me

twitter.com/packer_land

facebook.com/packerlandfans

joefletcher.net

CONTENTS

DEDICATION

This book is dedicated to Jill, who has lived up to her vow to be a Packers fan for life, with patience and understanding throughout football season, for nearly two decades.
My love, my life.

To my parents, Wayne and Maureen, die-hard Packer fans, who gave me the values, discipline, and sense of justice that has guided me my whole life.

To my bros, Scott and Nirish, as much as I look forward to our annual Packer trips, your friendship and endless support mean more than you'll ever know.

FOREWORD PASS

If you're reading this, chances are you or someone close to you is a loyal fan of the Green Bay Packers. I don't blame you – we are the real *America's Team*, right?

Notice I said *we*. As Packer fans, we tend to use the term "we". The Packers are a part of us, who we are, it's our identity. Heck, as a community-owned team, some of us are actual shareholders in the organization, me included.

Some of us have been waiting our whole lives to get season tickets. I'm number 65,156 on the waitlist as of this writing.

It's this love for the Packers, and history, that inspired me to write this quiz book.

My mission is two-fold.

First, that you thoroughly have fun showing off your hard-earned knowledge of obscure Packers trivia and relive some treasured NFL moments.

Second, that you come to appreciate this legendary team even more as you discover key facts you previously didn't know – as I did in writing this book.

Ok, it's time to kick this off. Go Pack Go!

MAKE IT A GAME

Whether you're reading this book by yourself, or challenging your friends and family, here are a few fun ways to turn these trivia questions into a game.

Team Formation

Solo Tackle

If you're playing alone, set a benchmark and see if you can meet it or beat it. Each chapter has 10 questions. Set a goal for how many you will answer correctly for each chapter.

Man Coverage

Two or more players with everyone playing for themselves – no teaming up. Each player takes turns answering a chapter's 10 questions. Whoever gets the most correct after each round wins that round.

Zone Coverage

If you have multiple players, you can form teams and try to balance out the experience level between teams. Each team takes turns answering 10 questions. Whichever team gets the most correct after each round wins that round.

Level the Playing Field

This book organizes the questions into 3 levels of difficulty. Level I is the easiest, Level II is medium, and Level III is the most difficult.

If you have players or teams with varying levels of Packers knowledge, consider having the more-knowledgeable players answer questions from higher levels.

Scoring Drive

Decide between awarding 1 point for every correct answer or assigning different point values based on the question's difficulty level.

Example Points per Correct Answer

Level I:	1 point
Level II:	3 points
Level III:	6 points

The End Zone

Here are 3 different ways to determine the winner. Decide ahead of time which method you will use and how many rounds you'll play.

1) Each round is a new game, so whoever scores the most points in a round, wins that game, or

2) Play several rounds, and whichever team wins the most rounds, wins the game, or

3) Play several rounds, and whichever team scores the most points, wins the game.

GAME-TIME DECISIONS

Don't let this sit on your shelf. Get the most out of this book. Here are 5 occasions to use this book you may not have thought of.

Trivia Night
See if you can get your local establishment to host a Packers Trivia Night. You've got everything you need right here in this book.

Road Trips
Whether you're headed up from Milwaukee to your Gold Package game in Green Bay or road-tripping to an away game, bring this book along to brush up on your Packers trivia along the way.

Holidays
Spending time with the in-laws? Arguing politics with your crazy uncle? Call an audible and challenge them to a game of Packers trivia. As a Packer fan, this is surely a more enjoyable way to pass the time.

Commercial Breaks
I don't know about you, but I'm on edge during Packer games, and waiting for commercials to end is painful. Grab this book off your coffee table and occupy your mind with a few trivial questions.

Tailgating
Not that you really need more to do while tailgating, but if you run out of brats to turn, cups to flip, or polkas to polka, now you can impress your friends with these amazing Packers trivia questions and prove how much of a fan you really are.

LEVEL I

Basic Packers Trivia

LEVEL II

Hard Core Packers Trivia

LEVEL III

Ultimate Die-Hard Packers Trivia

Packers in 1919

LEVEL I

Basic Packers Trivia

1

CHAPTER 1

1. **What was the name of the Packers when they joined the NFL?**

   A) Green Bay Whales
   B) Acme Packers
   C) Indian Packers
   D) Green Bay Calhouns

2. **Due to mid-game injury, which quarterback did Brett Favre replace?**

   A) Blair Kiel
   B) Anthony Dilweg
   C) Don Majkowski
   D) Randy Wright

3. **Who was the first head coach of the Packers?**

   A) George Whitney Calhoun
   B) Gene Ronzani
   C) Curly Lambeau
   D) Vince Lombardi

4. **Who was nicknamed the "Minister of Defense"?**

   A) Julius Peppers
   B) B.J. Raji
   C) Tim Harris
   D) Reggie White

5. **Which team have the Packers faced the most in NFL history?**

A) Los Angeles Rams
B) Detroit Lions
C) Chicago Bears
D) Minnesota Vikings

6. **How many NFL titles have the Packers won?**

A) 11
B) 4
C) 13
D) 5

7. **Which quarterback has the lowest interception rate in Packers history? (min. 100 passes)**

A) Matt Flynn
B) Blair Kiel
C) Jordan Love
D) Aaron Rodgers

8. **Which team did the Packers play in Super Bowl XLV (45)?**

A) Baltimore Ravens
B) New England Patriots
C) Pittsburgh Steelers
D) Indianapolis Colts

9. **What's the name of the play Lombardi made famous that involved pulling guards and a halfback "running to daylight"?**

A) Play Action Pass
B) I Formation
C) Bootleg
D) Packers Sweep

10. **Which game was known as "The Ice Bowl"?**

A) 1965 NFL Championship Game
B) 1967 NFL Championship Game
C) 1967 AFL-NFL World Championship Game
D) 1968 AFL-NFL World Championship Game

CHAPTER 1 ANSWERS

1. (B) Acme Packers

The original team sponsor, the Indian Packing Company, was bought by Acme Packing Co. of Chicago in 1920. The Indian Packers were renamed to the Acme Packers for the 1921 season when the team joined the NFL.

2. (C) Don Majkowski

In a 1992 game against the Cincinnati Bengals, Don Majkowski was forced out of the game with a torn ligament in his ankle. Brett Favre replaced him and led the Packers to a fourth-quarter comeback victory. Majkowski never started for Green Bay again and left for Indianapolis the following year, while Favre went on to start 297 consecutive games.

3. (C) Curly Lambeau

Technically, there was a head coach (in name only) named Willard Ryan in 1919. Curly Lambeau was team captain, however, and called plays and managed the team because football rules at the time prevented head coaches from talking to players during the game. Lambeau also co-founded the team, organized practices, and other duties that modern head coaches perform. As such, Lambeau is recognized as the Packers' first head coach.

4. (D) Reggie White

In addition to being an ordained minister, Reggie White was also the most valuable defensive player in NFL history according to Pro Football Reference (tied with Ray Lewis). White was Defensive Player of the Year twice, once as a Packer and once as an Eagle. "The Minister of Defense" retired #1 on the all-time sacks list with 198 sacks from 1985 to 2000.

5. (C) Chicago Bears

The Packers have faced the Chicago Bears 208 times, making it the most frequent matchup in NFL history. Surprisingly, the Bears and the Packers have only met 2 times in the playoffs. The Packers lead this historic rivalry 107-95-6.

6. (C) 13

The Packers have clinched the NFL Championship title 13 times, more than any other team in the league's history. This impressive tally includes victories in the pre-Super Bowl era as well as triumphs in Super Bowls I, II, XXXI (31), and XLV (45). Their first three championships were won consecutively from 1929 to 1931, and they achieved another three-peat from 1965 to 1967.

7. (D) Aaron Rodgers

Aaron Rodgers' career interception rate of 1.4% is the lowest in team history, and as of 2023, the lowest in NFL history. Jordan Love follows him with an interception rate of 2.1% as of 2023, Blair Kiel at 3.0%, and Matt Flynn at 3.2%.

8. (C) Pittsburgh Steelers

The Packers beat the Pittsburgh Steelers 31-25 in Super Bowl XLV (45), played at AT&T Stadium in 2011. This was Mike McCarthy's and Aaron Rodgers' first and only Super Bowl appearance for the Packers. Rodgers was awarded Super Bowl MVP for his performance, completing 24 of 39 passes for 304 yards and 3 TDs with 0 picks.

9. (D) Packers Sweep

The "Packers Sweep" became a signature play under coach Vince Lombardi. It utilized pulling guards such as Hall of Famer Jerry Kramer to create a path for the halfback, who would "run to daylight" exploiting holes in the defense. This strategic move helped solidify the Packers' dominance in the 1960s.

10. (B) 1967 NFL Championship Game

The 1967 NFL Championship Game, played on New Year's Eve at Lambeau Field, was known as "The Ice Bowl" due to sub-zero temperatures. It is still the coldest game ever played in the NFL. Packers linebacker Ray Nitschke got frostbite in his feet and lost his toenails. Several other Cowboys and Packers players suffered frostbite and flu-like symptoms during the game.

2

CHAPTER 2

1. **Who was head coach of the Packers before Ray Rhodes took over in 1999?**

   A) Lindy Infante
   B) Mike Holmgren
   C) Mike Sherman
   D) Andy Reid

2. **Which Packer's nickname was "Blood"?**

   A) Henry Jordan
   B) Chuck Cecil
   C) Johnny McNally
   D) Nick Barnett

3. **How did the Packers raise funds to keep the team going in 1923?**

   A) Mortgaged their stadium
   B) Solicited donations
   C) Sold stock
   D) Sold tickets

4. **Who has thrown for the most yards in Packers history?**

   A) Bart Starr
   B) Aaron Rodgers
   C) Brett Favre
   D) Lynn Dickey

5. **How many Super Bowl championships did Bart Starr lead the Packers to?**

   A) 3
   B) 2
   C) 4
   D) 1

6. **Which team did the Packers play in the first AFL-NFL World Championship Game?**

   A) Kansas City Chiefs
   B) Oakland Raiders
   C) Cleveland Browns
   D) New York Jets

7. **Who was the head coach of the Packers in the 1959 season?**

   A) Lisle Blackbourn
   B) Ray McLean
   C) Phil Bengston
   D) Vince Lombardi

8. **What is the name of the mixed-use development located near Lambeau Field?**

   A) Green Bay Gardens
   B) Packers Plaza
   C) Titletown District
   D) Lambeau Village

9. **Which Packer, after partying the night before, scored the first touchdown in the first Super Bowl ever?**

A) Max McGee
B) Red Mack
C) Jim Grabowski
D) Boyd Dowler

10. **Which head coach won the most World Championships?**

A) Mike Holmgren
B) Curly Lambeau
C) Mike McCarthy
D) Vince Lombardi

CHAPTER 2 ANSWERS

1. (B) Mike Holmgren

Mike Holmgren was head coach of the Packers from 1992 to 1998, where he won Super Bowl XXXI (31). He left Green Bay to become head coach of the Seattle Seahawks from 1999 to 2008. His last role in the NFL was as team President of the Cleveland Browns from 2010 to 2012.

2. (C) Johnny McNally

In 1922, John McNally and Ralph Hanson saw the name "Blood and Sand" on a movie theater marquee while riding McNally's motorcycle on the way to practice. In an attempt to maintain their college football eligibility at Notre Dame, from which they were kicked off the team, they adopted the pseudonyms "Blood" and "Sand" to obscure their names while playing pro football.

3. (C) Sold stock

In 1923, facing financial difficulties, the Packers devised an innovative solution to ensure the team's survival by selling stock to the public. This move was groundbreaking, transforming the Packers into a community-owned franchise, a unique status they maintain to this day. The sale of stock allowed fans to invest directly in the team's future, fostering a deep sense of ownership and loyalty among the community. This strategy not only stabilized the team financially but also cemented the Packers' position as a cherished institution in Green Bay.

4. (C) Brett Favre

In 16 seasons from 1992 to 2007, Brett Favre threw for 61,655 yards as a Packer. Aaron Rodgers threw for 59,055 yards in 18 seasons (15 as a starter), Bart Starr threw for 24,718 and Lynn Dickey threw for 21,369. Rodgers has the highest average with 257 yards per game compared to Favre's 242-yard average.

5. (B) 2

Bart Starr led the Packers to 5 NFL Championships, including victories in Super Bowl I and II. Throughout his career, Starr was known for his leadership and game management skills. In addition to his Super Bowl success, Starr was a four-time Pro Bowler and was named the NFL MVP in 1966. He led the league in passer rating five times and retired with the NFL's second-best career passer rating of 80.5.

6. (A) Kansas City Chiefs

In the inaugural AFL-NFL World Championship Game, now known as Super Bowl I, the Packers faced off against the Kansas City Chiefs. Held in 1967, this historic matchup marked the first time AFL and NFL teams competed for the ultimate title in American football. The Packers, led by MVP quarterback Bart Starr, emerged victorious, defeating the Chiefs with a final score of 35-10, setting the stage for what would become one of the most anticipated sporting events in the United States.

7. (D) Vince Lombardi

With losing records for 12 straight years, including a one-win season the year prior, the Packers hired Vince Lombardi in 1959. Lombardi immediately turned the team around with a winning season in his first year as head coach and general manager. Lombardi never had a losing season and till this day has the best winning percentage of any head coach in Packer history.

8. (C) Titletown District

Titletown is a mixed-use development located near Lambeau Field, launched by the Packers to enhance the area's appeal and provide year-round entertainment for both locals and visitors. This expansive project includes a public plaza, park activities, a hotel, a sports medicine clinic, and dining, retail, and residential spaces. Titletown aims to extend the community and fan experience beyond football season, fostering a vibrant atmosphere that celebrates the spirit and heritage of the Packers and the wider Green Bay community.

9. (A) Max McGee

Going into the game, McGee had only caught 4 passes all season and did not expect to play much in Super Bowl I. He had spent the previous night partying and allegedly got only 1 hour of sleep. When Boyd Dowler was injured early in the game, McGee went it, ending up with 7 catches for 138 yards and 2 touchdowns. His first touchdown was a one-handed grab that he turned into a 37-yard score, which was the first touchdown in Super Bowl history.

10. (B) Curly Lambeau

Curly Lambeau's Packers won 6 NFL Championships. The first three championships (1929, 1930, 1931) were determined by having the best record in the league because the NFL did not do playoff games to determine the champion until 1933. Lambeau's next three championships came in wins over the Boston Redskins in 1936 and the New York Giants in 1939 and 1944.

CHAPTER 3

1. **Which quarterback has thrown the most touchdowns in Packers history?**

   A) Aaron Rodgers
   B) Brett Favre
   C) Lynn Dickey
   D) Bart Starr

2. **What major change to Packer attire did head coach Gene Ronzani implement in 1950?**

   A) Helmet logos
   B) Blue and gold uniforms
   C) Helmet facemasks
   D) Green and gold uniforms

3. **What play did Bart Starr run for the game-winning touchdown in the 1967 NFL Championship Game?**

   A) Quarterback Sneak
   B) Hail Mary
   C) Flea Flicker
   D) Sweep

4. **What number did the Packers retire in honor of Reggie White?**

   A) 92
   B) 88
   C) 94
   D) 75

5. **Who was the first Green Bay Packer to have his number retired?**

   A) Tony Canadeo
   B) Bart Starr
   C) Don Hutson
   D) Ray Nitschke

6. **What position does Brian Gutekunst currently hold with the Packers?**

   A) General Manager
   B) Director of Personnel
   C) EVP Football Operations
   D) Executive Committee President

7. **How many regular season games did Matt LaFleur win in each of his first 3 seasons as head coach?**

   A) 13 games
   B) 11 games
   C) 14 games
   D) 12 games

8. **In what year did the Packers join the NFL?**

   A) 1918
   B) 1919
   C) 1920
   D) 1921

9. **What number did the Packers retire in honor of Brett Favre?**

A) 5
B) 4
C) 3
D) 15

10. **Who was the MVP of Super Bowl I?**

A) Bart Starr
B) Max McGee
C) Elijah Pitts
D) Jim Taylor

CHAPTER 3 ANSWERS

1.   (A) Aaron Rodgers

Aaron Rodgers has thrown the most touchdown passes as a Packer with 475. Brett Favre fired off 442 as a Packer, Bart Starr threw 152, and Lynn Dickey tossed 133.

2.   (D) Green and gold uniforms

Gene Ronzani, who became the Packers' second head coach, made a big change to the team's uniforms by moving away from the original blue and gold colors established by Curly Lambeau. Emphasizing the "Green", Ronzani stated "We are the 'Green' Bay Packers", and thus changed the uniforms to green and gold.

3.   (A) Quarterback Sneak

With seconds remaining in the 1967 NFL Championship "Ice Bowl", Bart Starr ran a goal-line quarterback sneak into the end zone for the game-winning touchdown. Starr's offensive linemen Jerry Kramer and Ken Bowman double-teamed the Cowboys defensive tackle to allow Starr to barely squeak in. Despite the brutally cold conditions, Starr's successful sneak is frozen in time as one of the NFL's most iconic moments.

4.   (A) 92

Reggie White is the only player to have his jersey number retired by two NFL teams - the Packers and the Philadelphia Eagles. His alma mater, the University of Tennessee, also retired #92. His legendary "hump move" routinely left offensive linemen in his wake, allowing him to rack up 198 sacks in 232 games over his career, including 3 sacks in Super Bowl XXXI (31).

5.   (C) Don Hutson

Don Hutson, a pioneering figure in the evolution of the wide receiver position and a prolific record-setter, was the first Packer to have his jersey number (#14) retired in 1951. Hutson's career with the Packers, spanning from 1935 to 1945, included leading the league in receiving eight times and setting multiple NFL records, some of which stood for decades.

6.   (A) General Manager

Brian Gutekunst became the general manager of the Packers in 2018, succeeding Ted Thompson. Prior to his promotion, Gutekunst served in various roles within the organization, beginning his career with the Packers in 1998 as a scouting intern before moving up the ranks.

7. (A) 13 games each season

Matt LaFleur led the Packers to 13 regular season wins in each of his first three years. In fact, this was the first time ever an NFL team won 13 regular season games in 3 consecutive years (2019, 2020, 2021). Through his first 40 regular-season games, LaFleur had the best start by any head coach in the Super Bowl era, going 33 - 7. LaFleur also broke a record, held by George Seifert for 3 decades, for the most wins in his first 3 seasons (39).

8. (D) 1921

In 1921, after two years of dominating local rivals, the Packers joined the American Professional Football Association, now known as the National Football League. The APFA had only played one season and had only 10 teams before the Packers joined. Of the 10, only the Decatur Staleys (Chicago Bears) and Chicago Cardinals (Arizona Cardinals) are still in the league today, which makes the Packers the third oldest team in the NFL.

9. (B) 4

Favre never missed a game as quarterback after starting for Green Bay from 1992 to 2007. As a Packer legend with a mountain of records, the team planned to retire his jersey number 4 in 2008. But after drama involving retiring, unretiring, and playing for the Jets and Vikings, the Packers held off until relationships had time to heal before retiring #4 in 2015.

10. (A) Bart Starr

In the first Super Bowl, Starr went 16 for 23 for 250 yards, 2 TDs, 1 INT, and a 116.2 passer rating. Max McGee, who had only caught 4 passes all season, caught 7 receptions for 138 yards and 2 TDs. Jim Taylor had 17 carries for 56 yards, and Elijah Pitts had 11 carries for 45 yards.

CHAPTER 4

1. **Which team did the Packers defeat in the 2023 Wild Card playoff game?**

   A) Detroit Lions
   B) Dallas Cowboys
   C) San Francisco 49ers
   D) Los Angeles Rams

2. **How many Super Bowls has Mike McCarthy won as head coach of the Packers?**

   A) 0
   B) 1
   C) 2
   D) 3

3. **Besides Lombardi, who is the only other non-player Packer to be enshrined in the Pro Football Hall of Fame?**

   A) Ron Wolf
   B) Ted Thompson
   C) Bob Harlan
   D) Mike Holmgren

4. **How many interceptions were returned for touchdowns in Super Bowl XLV (45)?**

   A) 2
   B) 3
   C) 0
   D) 1

5. **Who has the longest kickoff return in Packers history?**

A) Keisean Nixon
B) Travis Williams
C) Al Carmichael
D) Randall Cobb

6. **How many Packers have had their jersey number retired?**

A) 8
B) 9
C) 7
D) 6

7. **Which of these coaches has never earned the AP NFL Coach of the Year award?**

A) Vince Lombardi
B) Mike McCarthy
C) Lindy Infante
D) Mike Holmgren

8. **What is the cool nickname Lambeau Field is often called?**

A) Fortress of Frost
B) The Tundra Temple
C) Frostbite Field
D) The Frozen Tundra

9. **How many NFL MVP awards has Brett Favre won?**

   A) 4
   B) 3
   C) 1
   D) 2

10. **Which player was the first and only Packer to have his number retired posthumously?**

   A) Tony Canadeo
   B) Don Hutson
   C) Ray Nitschke
   D) Reggie White

CHAPTER 4 ANSWERS

1.   (B) Dallas Cowboys

The Packers were the first #7 seed to ever win a game in NFL history, beating the #2 seeded Cowboys coached by former Packer head coach, Mike McCarthy. The Packers started 27-0 before finishing 48-32, preserving their undefeated record at AT&T Stadium. Love had ended the playoff game with a perfect passer rating (Wikipedia had even added him as just the fifth QB to ever achieve this), but as their lead narrowed, he came back in and threw one incomplete pass to ruin his perfect rating.

2.   (B) 1

Mike McCarthy served as the head coach of the Packers and led the team to a Super Bowl XLV (45) victory in 2011. This win was McCarthy's only Super Bowl championship for the Packers, beating the Pittsburgh Steelers with a final score of 31-25. This win was the Packers' fourth Super Bowl title in the franchise's history.

3.   (A) Ron Wolf

Ron Wolf is the only non-player from the team, aside from Vince Lombardi, to be inducted into the Pro Football Hall of Fame. His moves to trade for Brett Favre and acquire Reggie White in free agency reversed decades of losing and set the team on the path to decades of championship-caliber play. Since acquiring Favre in 1992, the Packers have the 2nd best record in the NFL.

4.   (D) 1

In Super Bowl XLV (45), Nick Collins, a safety for the Packers, intercepted a pass from Ben Roethlisberger, the quarterback of the Pittsburgh Steelers, and returned it 37 yards for a pick-six touchdown in the first quarter. Following the play, he received a 15-yard penalty for excessive celebration.

5.   (D) Randall Cobb

In 2011, in his first NFL game, Cobb returned a kick deep in his end zone for 108 yards. In 1956, Al Carmichael returned a kick for 106 yards. In 2022, Keisean Nixon returned a kick 105 yards and was named first-team All-Pro as a kick returner. In 1967, Travis Williams had a 104-yard return.

6.   (D) 6

Six Packers have had their jersey numbers retired and displayed in the ring of honor at Lambeau Field: Tony Canadeo (#3), Brett Favre (#4), Don Hutson (#14), Bart Starr (#15), Ray Nitschke (#66), and Reggie White (#92).

7. (D) Mike Holmgren

Mike Holmgren, who was the head coach of the Packers from 1992 to 1998, led the team to two Super Bowl appearances, including winning Super Bowl XXXI (31). Despite his success with the Packers and his influence in the NFL during the 1990s, Holmgren never received the AP NFL Coach of the Year award. His time with the Packers is noted for revitalizing the team from decades of malaise, but he did not receive this particular award during his career as a head coach.

8. (D) The Frozen Tundra

The Frozen Tundra nickname emanated from the 1967 Ice Bowl where the field was nearly more ice than grass. The underground heating system, installed prior to that season, was not powerful enough to counteract the sub-zero temperatures during the game.

9. (B) 3

Hall of Famer Brett Favre won the NFL Most Valuable Player award three years in a row, from 1995 to 1997.

10. (D) Reggie White

Reggie White, who passed away a year earlier, had his jersey number (#92) retired in 2005. White was a two-time NFL Defensive Player of the Year, 13-time Pro Bowler, 10-time All-Pro first team, and Super Bowl XXXI (31) champion. He retired as the all-time NFL sack leader and was inducted into the Pro Football Hall of Fame in 2006.

CHAPTER 5

1. **How many Super Bowls have the Packers lost?**

    A) 1
    B) 3
    C) 7
    D) 5

2. **Which Packer has caught the most touchdowns?**

    A) Jordy Nelson
    B) Davante Adams
    C) Don Hutson
    D) Sterling Sharpe

3. **What was quarterback Don Majkowski's nickname?**

    A) The Holy Macowsky
    B) The Mack Daddy
    C) The Majik Man
    D) The Don

4. **How many Super Bowls have the Packers won?**

    A) 13
    B) 4
    C) 6
    D) 5

5. **Who was the general manager of the Packers before Brian Gutekunst?**

A) Ron Wolf
B) Bob Harlan
C) Ted Thompson
D) Mike Sherman

6. **How many times did Aaron Rodgers win the NFL MVP award?**

A) 4
B) 5
C) 2
D) 3

7. **Who was the Packers quarterback that broke Dan Marino's NFL record for passing yards?**

A) Aaron Rodgers
B) Brett Favre
C) Bart Starr
D) Lynn Dickey

8. **In what year were the Packers founded?**

A) 1925
B) 1915
C) 1919
D) 1921

9. **Who was the head coach of the Packers during Super Bowl II?**

   A) Bill Walsh
   B) Vince Lombardi
   C) Tom Landry
   D) Chuck Noll

10. **What is the name of the Packer's indoor practice facility?**

    A) Don Hutson Center
    B) Packers Athletic Center Komplex (PACK)
    C) Bellin Practice Fields
    D) Titletown Tryout Facility

CHAPTER 5 ANSWERS

1. (A) 1

The Packers are 4 - 1 in Super Bowls, having only lost to the John Elway led Denver Broncos in Super Bowl XXXII (32).

2. (C) Don Hutson

Don Hutson, playing from 1935 to 1945, recorded 99 touchdown receptions, 3 rushing touchdowns, 1 interception return for a touchdown, and 2 return touchdowns. His total of 105 touchdowns makes him the Packers' all-time touchdown leader. Following Hutson in touchdown receptions are Davante Adams with 73, Jordy Nelson with 69, and Sterling Sharpe with 65.

3. (C) The Majik Man

Don Majkowski, known as "The Majik Man," captivated Packer fans in the late 1980s with his dynamic play and ability to orchestrate come-from-behind victories. His standout season came in 1989 when he led the NFL in passing yards and helped the Packers to a winning record, earning a Pro Bowl selection in the process.

4.   (B) 4

The Packers have won 4 Super Bowls: I, II, XXXI (31), and XLV (45) following the 1966, 1967, 1996, and 2010 seasons respectively. They won 3 NFL Championships by league standing (having the best overall record) and 6 NFL Championship games before the AFL-NFL merger. In total, the Packers have won 13 NFL Championships, more than any other team.

5.   (C) Ted Thompson

Before Brian Gutekunst assumed the role, Ted Thompson served as the general manager of the Packers. Thompson's tenure was marked by a philosophy of building the team through the draft, a strategy that paid dividends by assembling a roster that won Super Bowl XLV (45). His decision to draft Aaron Rodgers in 2005 stands out as a pivotal move, ensuring the team's competitive edge for years.

6.   (A) 4

Aaron Rodgers has been named Most Valuable Player 4 times. Only Peyton Manning has more, winning the award 5 times. Tom Brady, Brett Favre, Johnny Unitas, and Jim Brown have each won the award 3 times.

7.   (B) Brett Favre

It took Dan Marino 17 seasons to pass for 61,361 yards. At age 38 in his 17th season, Brett Favre surpassed that mark with a simple 7-yard slant to Donald Driver. Favre ended his career with 61,655 yards for the Packers and 71,838 yards overall.

8. (C) 1919

The Packers were founded in 1919, two years before joining the NFL in 1921. The team was started by Earl "Curly" Lambeau and George Calhoun, who decided to form a professional football team that was financially supported by Lambeau's employer, the Indian Packing Company.

9. (B) Vince Lombardi

Vince Lombardi was the head coach of the Packers during Super Bowl II, leading the team to victory over the Oakland Raiders. This win not only secured the Packers' second consecutive Super Bowl title but also marked Lombardi's final game as the team's head coach.

10. (A) Don Hutson Center

Located across the street from Lambeau Field, the Don Hutson Center is the indoor practice facility for the Packers. It includes both a 70-yard practice field and a 60-yarder, allowing the offense and defense to practice at the same time. In addition to the Hutson Center, the Packers have 2 outdoor practice fields, the Ray Nitschke Field and Clarke Hinkle Field.

6

CHAPTER 6

1. **Which Packer punt returner scored the most touchdowns in a single season?**

   A) Billy Grimes
   B) Will Blackmon
   C) Micah Hyde
   D) Desmond Howard

2. **Which quarterback led the Packers to victory in Super Bowl II?**

   A) Bart Starr
   B) Brett Favre
   C) Aaron Rodgers
   D) Joe Montana

3. **What was the capacity of the original City Stadium when the Packers first started playing there in 1925?**

   A) 22,000
   B) 6,000
   C) 14,000
   D) 9,000

4. **Who is the winningest coach in Packers history?**

   A) Vince Lombardi
   B) Mike McCarthy
   C) Curly Lambeau
   D) Mike Holmgren

5. **Which quarterback has thrown the most interceptions in Packers history?**

   A) Lynn Dickey
   B) Tobin Rote
   C) Brett Favre
   D) Bart Starr

6. **Which team did the Packers play in the second AFL-NFL World Championship Game?**

   A) Oakland Raiders
   B) New York Jets
   C) Kansas City Chiefs
   D) Miami Dolphins

7. **Who passed Sterling Sharpe to become second in all-time Packer receptions?**

   A) Davante Adams
   B) Randall Cobb
   C) Jordy Nelson
   D) Donald Driver

8. **What number did the Packers retire in honor of Tony Canadeo?**

   A) 3
   B) 66
   C) 14
   D) 15

9. **Who was named MVP of Super Bowl XLV (45)?**

A) Desmond Howard
B) Aaron Rodgers
C) Clay Matthews
D) Charles Woodson

10. **Which Packer has been sacked the most often?**

A) Brett Favre
B) Bart Starr
C) Aaron Rodgers
D) Lynn Dickey

CHAPTER 6 ANSWERS

1. (D) Desmond Howard

Desmond Howard scored 3 touchdowns while returning punts for the Packers in 1996. He set the NFL record for most punt return yards with 875, a mark that he still holds today. He led the NFL with 58 punt returns that season, still the most by any Packer and third in NFL history.

2. (A) Bart Starr

Bart Starr led the Packers to their second consecutive Super Bowl win and third NFL Championship in a row. Starr's offense scored 17 unanswered points in the second half to end the day 33-14 over the Raiders. Starr completed 13 of 24 passes for 202 yards, including a 62-yard touchdown to Boyd Dowler. Starr was named Super Bowl MVP, his second such award in 2 years.

3. (B) 6,000

When the Packers first started playing at the original City Stadium in 1925, the venue had a capacity of just 6,000 fans, expanding to 25,000 by the time they played their last game there after 32 seasons. The players used nearby Green Bay East High School for their lockers, but visiting teams had to use their hotel before the game, usually at Hotel Northland. Today, the school uses City Stadium for their playing field.

4.   (C) Curly Lambeau

Curly Lambeau is the winningest coach in Packers' history, with a record of 209 wins, 104 losses, and 21 ties. Second all-time is Mike McCarthy with 125 wins, followed by Vince Lombardi with 89 wins and Mike Holmgren with 75 wins. Including his time in Chicago and Washington, Lambeau ranks 6th among the NFL's all-time winningest coaches.

5.   (C) Brett Favre

Known as an aggressive gunslinger, Brett Favre has the record for the most interceptions thrown by a Packer with 286 over his 16 seasons with the team. Lynn Dickey had 151, Bart Starr had 138, and Tobin Rote had 119. Favre still holds the NFL all-time record for passing interceptions with 336.

6.   (A) Oakland Raiders

In the second AFL-NFL World Championship Game, now known as Super Bowl II, the Packers beat the Oakland Raiders 33-14. This was Lombardi's fifth NFL title, and his last game as head coach of the Packers. The Raiders came into the game with a regular season record of 13-1 and had just defeated the Houston Oilers 40-7 in the AFL Championship Game. The Packers were just 9-4-1 during the season, but the 2-time defending NFL champs dominated the Raiders on their way to their 3rd straight NFL title.

7. (A) Davante Adams

Davante Adams surpassed Sterling Sharpe to become second in all-time Packer receptions, amassing a total of 669 catches over his 8 years with the Packers. Adams led the Packers in receptions and receiving yards five straight years, from 2017 to 2021.

8. (A) 3

When Tony Canadeo retired as the Packers all-time leading rusher, his jersey number 3 was retired as well. He led the Packers in rushing 5 different seasons and was the third NFL player to ever rush for more than 1,000 yards in a season. Canadeo's career was interrupted by serving in World War II in both the Navy and the Army, missing most of 1944 and 1945 NFL seasons.

9. (B) Aaron Rodgers

Aaron Rodgers was named MVP of Super Bowl XLV (45) after leading the Packers to victory against the Pittsburgh Steelers. Rodgers was 24 of 39, passing for 304 yards, 3 touchdowns, no interceptions, and was just the third quarterback to pass for over 1,000 yards in one postseason.

10. (C) Aaron Rodgers

Aaron Rodgers is the most sacked Packer in history, having been taken down 530 times in 230 games played from 2005 to 2022. His sacks-per-attempt percentage is 6.5% compared to Favre's 4.8%, who was sacked just 438 times. Jordan Love has the lowest sack percentage of all Packers franchise QBs at 4.7%, albeit just a one season sample (2023).

Jim Taylor, Paul Hornung, Bart Starr, & Vince Lombardi at Super Bowl I

LEVEL II

Hard Core Packers Trivia

7

CHAPTER 7

1. **Who is the all-time leading rusher for the Packers?**

   A) Jim Taylor
   B) John Brockington
   C) Ahman Green
   D) Aaron Jones

2. **What primary position did Ray Nitschke play in the NFL?**

   A) Linebacker
   B) Safety
   C) Nose Tackle
   D) Defensive end

3. **Who was named MVP of Super Bowl XXXI (31)?**

   A) Desmond Howard
   B) Antonio Freeman
   C) Brett Favre
   D) Reggie White

4. **Which Packer surpassed Sterling Sharpe for most catches as a rookie?**

   A) Billy Howton
   B) Gerry Ellis
   C) Jayden Reed
   D) Christian Watson

5. What college hosted the Packers training camp from 1958 to 2019?

A) Beloit College
B) St. Norbert College
C) Ripon College
D) Bellin College

6. Who was named the NFL's MVP for the 1995 season?

A) Brett Favre
B) John Elway
C) Troy Aikman
D) Dan Marino

7. Which Packer had the most career receiving yards per game on average?

A) Davante Adams
B) Sterling Sharpe
C) James Lofton
D) Billy Howton

8. Who has the most pick-six interceptions as a Packer?

A) Darren Sharper
B) Charles Woodson
C) Herb Adderley
D) Bobby Dillon

9. **Which running back also made 66 field goals as a Packer?**

   A) John Brockington
   B) Paul Hornung
   C) Tony Canadeo
   D) Clarke Hinkle

10. **Who was the head coach of the Dallas Cowboys for their matchup with the Packers in the 1967 "Ice Bowl"?**

   A) Chuck Knoll
   B) George Halas
   C) Don Shula
   D) Tom Landry

CHAPTER 7 ANSWERS

1. (C) Ahman Green

Ahman Green stands as the all-time leading rusher for the Packers, accumulating 8,322 yards on 1,851 attempts over 10 seasons from 2000 to 2009. In fact, Green has the longest run as a Packer (98 yards), most rushing yards in a single game (218 yards), and most yards in a single season (1,883 yards in 2003).

2. (A) Linebacker

Ray Nitschke played linebacker from 1958 to 1972 for the Packers and was considered to be the best linebacker in NFL history when he was named to the NFL's 50th Anniversary team. He's also the only linebacker to be named to both the 50th and 75th Anniversary teams. He's the only Lombardi-era player besides Bart Starr to have his jersey number retired. The Packers named one of their practice facilities "Ray Nitschke Field" is his honor in 1997.

3. (A) Desmond Howard

Desmond Howard is the only player in Super Bowl history to win the MVP without a single play on offense or defense. He won the MVP by setting 5 Super Bowl special teams records for most punt returns (6), most punt return yards (90), most return yards (244), most kickoff returns for a touchdown (1), and longest kickoff return (99 yards).

4.   (C) Jayden Reed

Jayden Reed caught 64 passes as a rookie during his 2023 season with the Packers. Before Reed, the Packers record for most receptions by a rookie was held by Sterling Sharpe, who caught 55 passes in 1988.

5.   (B) St. Norbert College

St. Norbert College hosted the Packers training camp from 1958 to 2019, a tradition started by Vince Lombardi. For three weeks each summer, the players would stay in the college dorms, and it was common to see local area kids helping out Packer legends such as Starr, Hornung, and Nitschke get their chores done. Pandemic restrictions in 2020 broke the tradition, and the Packers now use their facilities at Lambeau Field for all their training camp activities.

6.   (A) Brett Favre

Brett Favre won the first of his 3 MVP awards in 1995, the year before his first Super Bowl season. Favre threw for 38 touchdowns, 13 picks, 4,413 yards, and a 99.5 passer rating in that season.

7.   (B) Sterling Sharpe

Sterling Sharpe leads the Pack with the most career receiving yards on average with 72.6 yards per game. He's followed by James Lofton with 71 receiving yards per game, Davante Adams with 70 yards per game, and Billy Howton with 69.8 yards per game.

8. (B) Charles Woodson

The Packers have 149 pick-sixes all-time as of the conclusion of the 2023 season. Charles Woodson leads the Pack with the most interceptions returned for a touchdown with 9. Herb Adderley had 7. Bobby Dillon and Darren Sharper each had 5.

9. (B) Paul Hornung

Paul Hornung is best known for his running back duties, but he also kicked field goals. In his career as a Packer, he made 66 field goals on 140 attempts. In 1960, he set the NFL scoring record by combining his rushing touchdowns, field goals, and extra points to score 176 points. That record stood until 2006 when LaDainian Tomlinson scored 30 touchdowns for 180 points.

10. (D) Tom Landry

Tom Landry vs. Vince Lombardi in the 1967 Ice Bowl remains one of the most iconic head coaching matchups in NFL history. The two legends previously coached together on the same Giants team (Landry as defensive coordinator and Lombardi as offensive coordinator) before leaving to become head coaches of their respective teams. Landry lost this matchup but went on to coach the Cowboys to wins in Super Bowl VI and XII.

CHAPTER 8

1. **Which team did the Packers defeat in the 1967 NFL Championship Game?**

   A) Los Angeles Rams
   B) Cleveland Browns
   C) Kansas City Chiefs
   D) Dallas Cowboys

2. **Who is the all-time leading scorer for the Packers?**

   A) Brett Favre
   B) Ryan Longwell
   C) Mason Crosby
   D) Aaron Rodgers

3. **Which receiver did Donald Driver pass to become the all-time reception yardage leader for the Packers?**

   A) Sterling Sharpe
   B) Boyd Dowler
   C) Don Hutson
   D) James Lofton

4. **Why were the Packers kicked out of the NFL in 1922?**

   A) Financial instability issues
   B) Playing college players
   C) Illegal game tactics
   D) Signing high school players

5. **Which Packer holds the lead for most catches per game on average?**

A) Greg Jennings
B) Jayden Reed
C) Jordy Nelson
D) Davante Adams

6. **How many Super Bowl MVP awards did Bart Starr win?**

A) 3
B) 2
C) 1
D) 0

7. **Which team did the Packers beat in the NFC Championship game to advance to Super Bowl XLV (45)?**

A) Atlanta Falcons
B) Philadelphia Eagles
C) San Francisco 49ers
D) Chicago Bears

8. **Who caught Brett Favre's 400th touchdown?**

A) Greg Jennings
B) Antonio Freeman
C) Donald Driver
D) Jordy Nelson

9. **What position did Arnie Herber play in the NFL?**

A) Running Back
B) Quarterback
C) Cornerback
D) Wide Receiver

10. **Which team did the Packers defeat for their first NFL Championship title?**

A) New York Giants
B) No championship game played
C) Chicago Bears
D) Detroit Lions

CHAPTER 8 ANSWERS

1. (D) Dallas Cowboys

The Packers emerged victorious over the Dallas Cowboys in the iconic "Ice Bowl". The win against the Cowboys advanced the Packers to Super Bowl II, where they clinched another title.

2. (C) Mason Crosby

Mason Crosby holds the title of all-time leading scorer for the Packers, accumulating 1,918 points over 15 seasons. His scoring record includes 395 field goals and 733 extra points. Other top scorers include Ryan Longwell with 1,054 points, Don Hutson with 825, Chris Jacke with 820, Paul Hornung with 760, and Jim Taylor with 546.

3. (D) James Lofton

During his 9 seasons as a Packer, James Lofton played in 7 Pro Bowls and left as the team's all-time leading receiver with 9,656 yards. Lofton was drafted #6 overall by the Packers in 1978 and inducted into the Pro Football Hall of Fame in 2003.

4. (B) Playing college players

In the 1921 "state championship" against the Racine Legion, the Packers fielded college players from Notre Dame using fake names - two moves that were against league rules. The NFL expelled the Packers at their annual meeting in Canton in January 1922, but reinstated the team by June, so they never missed a season.

5. (D) Davante Adams

Davante Adams leads all Packers with an average of 5.8 receptions per game, followed by Sterling Sharpe with 5.3 catches on average, Greg Jennings with 4.4, Don Hutson with 4.2, and Randall Cobb with 4.1. Jayden Reed (2023) and Jordy Nelson each averaged 4 catches per game.

6. (B) 2

Bart Starr was named Most Valuable Player in Super Bowl II, making him a back-to-back Super Bowl MVP, a feat that only Terry Bradshaw and Patrick Mahomes have since achieved.

7. (D) Chicago Bears

The Packers, with a regular season record of 10-6, made history as the first NFC sixth-seed team to advance to the Super Bowl. Their journey to Super Bowl XLV (45) was marked by victories over the conference's top three seeded teams: the Philadelphia Eagles, the Atlanta Falcons, and the Chicago Bears in the NFC Conference game.

8. (A) Greg Jennings

Greg Jennings caught Favre's 400th touchdown, 420th touchdown to tie Dan Marino's record, 421st touchdown to break the record, and Aaron Rodgers' first-ever touchdown.

9. (B) Quarterback

Arnie Herber excelled as a quarterback for the Packers during the 1930s and early 1940s, becoming one of the NFL's first great passers. His powerful arm and keen vision on the field helped revolutionize the passing game in an era dominated by the run. Herber's partnership with receiver Don Hutson formed one of the most lethal aerial combinations of their time, contributing significantly to the Packers' early championship successes.

10. (B) No championship game played

The Packers secured their first NFL Championship in 1929, a time when the league did not hold a championship game to determine the title. Instead, the championship was awarded to the team with the best regular-season record. The 1929 championship was the first of three consecutive titles for the Packers.

9

CHAPTER 9

1. **What was the price per share during the 2021 stock sale for the Packers?**

   A) $300
   B) $200
   C) $250
   D) $350

2. **Which Packer kicker had a perfect regular season kicking field goals? (min. 10 attempts)**

   A) Max Zendejas
   B) Jan Stenerud
   C) Ryan Longwell
   D) Mason Crosby

3. **Who caught Aaron Rodgers' game-winning Hail Mary pass in Detroit in 2015?**

   A) Andrew Quarles
   B) James Jones
   C) Randall Cobb
   D) Richard Rodgers

4. **Which two receivers share the team record for most touchdown receptions in a single season?**

   A) Sterling Sharpe & Don Hutson
   B) Sterling Sharpe & Jordy Nelson
   C) Don Hutson & Davante Adams
   D) Sterling Sharpe & Davante Adams

5. **Who has the longest touchdown run as a Packer?**

    A) James Lofton
    B) Ahman Green
    C) Andy Uram
    D) Jim Taylor

6. **Which Packer holds the NFL record for most fumbles?**

    A) Aaron Rodgers
    B) Bart Starr
    C) Brett Favre
    D) Lynn Dickey

7. **How many seasons did the Packers play before officially joining the NFL?**

    A) 3
    B) 7
    C) 5
    D) 2

8. **Which head coach has the highest winning percentage all-time in Packers history?**

    A) Curly Lambeau
    B) Matt LaFleur
    C) Mike McCarthy
    D) Vince Lombardi

9. **Who was the Packers' first round draft choice that Sports Illustrated later called "The NFL's Incredible Bust"?**

    A) Rich Campbell
    B) Tony Mandarich
    C) Damarious Randall
    D) Terrell Buckley

10. **How many touchdowns did Brett Favre throw against the Raiders the night after his dad passed away?**

    A) 3
    B) 5
    C) 6
    D) 4

CHAPTER 9 ANSWERS

1. (A) 300

During the 2021 stock sale, shares in the Packers were offered at a price of $300 each. This marked one of the rare occasions when fans and supporters had the opportunity to own a piece of the storied NFL franchise. The sale was part of the Packers' exclusive ownership structure, where fans can invest in the organization, strengthening the bond between the community and the team. Proceeds from the sale were earmarked for improvements at Lambeau Field, including new video boards and concourse upgrades, ensuring the stadium remains a top-tier facility for fans and players alike.

2. (D) Mason Crosby

Mason Crosby achieved a perfect regular season in field goal attempts during the 2020 season, going 16 for 16. Crosby also led the NFL with 59 extra points made out of 63 attempts.

3. (D) Richard Rodgers

With 0 seconds on the clock due to a Detroit defensive penalty, Aaron Rodgers completed a 61-yard pass to the end zone, where Richard Rodgers made the game-winning catch to secure a 27-23 victory. This Rodgers-to-Rodgers Hail Mary is known as the "Miracle of Motown".

4. (D) Sterling Sharpe & Davante Adams

Sterling Sharpe (1994) and Davante Adams (2020) each caught 18 touchdowns in a single season. Hutson's best season was 17 touchdown receptions in an 11-game season in 1942, and Jordy Nelson's best was a 15-touchdown season in 2011.

5. (B) Ahman Green

Against the Denver Broncos in 2003, Ahman Green set team rushing records for the longest run (98 yards) and most yards in a game (218 yards). While at Nebraska, Green also set the Orange Bowl single game rushing record with 206 yards in the Husker's 1997 National Championship win over Tennessee.

6. (C) Brett Favre

Brett Favre holds the NFL record for most fumbles with a total of 166 - more than Warren Moon's 161 and Dave Krieg's 153. This statistic reflects the aggressive and fearless style that defined him as one of the game's most exciting quarterbacks. Despite this record, Favre's career included a Super Bowl win and three MVP awards.

7. (D) 2

The Packers were founded in 1919 and played 2 seasons of professional football before joining the NFL in 1921. Almost all of these games were blowout home games played at Hagemeister Park, with scores as high as 87-0 against Sheboygan. Teams from across Wisconsin, Michigan, and Chicago traveled to Green Bay, with only 4 away games in 2 seasons.

8. (D) Vince Lombardi

Vince Lombardi boasts the highest winning percentage all-time in Packers history, with a .754 winning percentage from 1959 to 1967, compiling a record of 89-29-4. Matt LaFleur, as of 2023, has the second highest percentage at .675. Mike Holmgren's winning percentage was .670, Curly Lambeau was .657, and Mike McCarthy was .556.

9. (B) Tony Mandarich

Tony Mandarich, the Packers' first-round draft choice, was later dubbed "The NFL's Incredible Bust" on the cover of Sports Illustrated. Mandarich's tenure with the Packers lasted just three unremarkable seasons, during which his performance fell far short of the expectations set for him as the second overall pick in the 1989 NFL draft. The Packers missed the opportunity to select future Hall of Famers Barry Sanders, Derrick Thomas, Deion Sanders, or Steve Atwater, making Mandarich's selection one of the most notable draft misses in NFL history.

10. (D) 4

In an emotional, magical performance with receivers completing unbelievable catches, Favre threw 4 touchdowns in the first half and finished the night 22 of 30 for 399 yards for a near perfect passer rating of 154.9.

CHAPTER 10

1. **Who is the officially recognized all-time sack leader for the Packers?**

   A) Willie Davis
   B) Clay Matthews
   C) Ezra Johnson
   D) Kabeer Gbaja-Biamila

2. **What are the most touchdowns Aaron Rodgers has thrown in a season?**

   A) 48
   B) 42
   C) 46
   D) 44

3. **Which head coach took the Packers to the most playoff games?**

   A) Mike Holmgren
   B) Curly Lambeau
   C) Mike McCarthy
   D) Vince Lombardi

4. **In Super Bowl 45, which coach motivated Clay Matthews to step up by telling him "It is time."?**

   A) Mike McCarthy
   B) Kevin Greene
   C) Dom Capers
   D) Winston Moss

5. **Who held the team record for most receptions in a season before Davante Adams caught 115 in 2020?**

A) Robert Brooks
B) Davante Adams
C) Sterling Sharpe
D) Jordy Nelson

6. **Which Packer caught the longest touchdown pass in Packer history?**

A) Sterling Sharpe
B) Antonio Freeman
C) Marquez Valdes-Scantling
D) Robert Brooks

7. **What number did the Packers retire in honor of Ray Nitschke?**

A) 66
B) 15
C) 63
D) 92

8. **Which Punter played the most games for the Packers?**

A) David Beverly
B) Don Bracken
C) Tim Masthay
D) Donny Anderson

9. **In what season did Aaron Rodgers set the NFL single-season passer rating at 122.5?**

A) 2011
B) 2020
C) 2021
D) 2014

10. **Which Packers team scored the most points in Packers history?**

A) The 2007 Packers
B) The 2014 Packers
C) The 1996 Packers
D) The 2011 Packers

CHAPTER 10 ANSWERS

1. (B) Clay Matthews

Clay Matthews is officially recognized by the Packers as their all-time sack leader with 83.5 regular season sacks from 2009 to 2018. However, this is based on official NFL stats which only started recording sacks in 1982. According to Pro Football Reference, which has unofficial sack stats back to 1960, Willie Davis leads the Packers with 99.5 sacks from 1960 to 1969.

2. (A) 48

In 2020, Aaron Rodgers threw 48 touchdowns, helping him earn his 3rd MVP that season. The Packers scored 30 or more points in all but 4 regular season games, and scored 509 points in total, second only to their 2011 season.

3. (C) Mike McCarthy

From 2006 to 2018, Mike McCarthy's Packers appeared in 18 playoff games. McCarthy was 10-8 in the postseason, including a win in Super Bowl XLV (45). McCarthy was fired during the 2018 season after failing to make the playoffs for 2 consecutive years.

4.   (B) Kevin Greene

After Charles Woodson broke his collarbone in Super Bowl XVL, Kevin Greene, the outside linebackers coach for the Packers, implored Clay Matthews with the words, "Everybody looks up to Wood as being a leader. He's gone. Nobody's standing up rallying the troops. It is time. It is time." Inspired by Greene's motivational words, Matthews stepped up in a critical moment, forcing a fumble that was recovered by Desmond Bishop. This pivotal play helped shift the momentum back to the Packers and contributed significantly to their victory over the Pittsburgh Steelers.

5.   (C) Sterling Sharpe

In 1993, Sterling Sharpe set an NFL record by catching 112 passes, breaking his own NFL record of 107 catches the year before. Sharpe's record stood for 27 years before Adams surpassed him in 2020.

6.   (D) Robert Brooks

Robert Brooks caught the longest touchdown pass in Packers history, a 99-yarder from Brett Favre, to beat the Bears on Monday Night in 1995.

7.   (A) 66

One of six numbers retired by the Packers, Ray Nitschke's number 66 has been permanently immortalized on the ring of honor at Lambeau Field. Nitschke spent his entire 15-year career as a Packer and won 5 NFL titles, 2 Super Bowls, was selected as an All-Pro 7 times, was named to the NFL 1960s All-Decade Team, 50th Anniversary Team, 75th Anniversary Team, and enshrined in the Pro Football Hall of Fame. Originally a Bears fan as a kid, Nitschke grew into one of the most iconic Packers of all time.

8.   (C) Tim Masthay

Tim Masthay holds the distinction of playing the most games as a punter for the Packers, appearing in 96 games from 2010 to 2015.

9.   (A) 2011

Aaron Rodgers' best season as a passer came in 2011 when he set the NFL single-season passer rating record at 122.5%. He almost met that mark again in 2020 with a 121.5% rating. 2014 and 2021 were his other top seasons with ratings of 112.2% and 111.9% respectively. As of 2023, Rodgers still has the best all-time NFL career passer rating at 103.6%, just ahead of Patrick Mahomes with 103.5%.

10. (D) The 2011 Packers

On the way to their best-ever regular season record of 15-1, the 2011 Packers set a franchise record by scoring 560 points. Only 3 other teams have scored more in NFL history: the 2013 Broncos with 606, the 2007 Patriots with 589, and the 2018 Chiefs with 565. None of those teams won the Super Bowl that year, and the Packers were knocked out of the postseason in their first playoff appearance.

11

CHAPTER 11

1. **How many NFL MVP awards has Bart Starr won?**

   A) 1
   B) 0
   C) 2
   D) 3

2. **Which Packers quarterback has the highest passer rating in a playoff game?**

   A) Lynn Dickey
   B) Aaron Rodgers
   C) Brett Favre
   D) Jordan Love

3. **Who is the only player in Packers history to wear #1 on their jersey?**

   A) Bart Starr
   B) No player ever
   C) Curly Lambeau
   D) Vince Lombardi

4. **Who is the all-time leading receiver for the Packers?**

   A) Davante Adams
   B) Donald Driver
   C) Sterling Sharpe
   D) Jordy Nelson

5. **Which team have the Packers faced the most in the playoffs?**

A) Los Angeles Rams
B) Dallas Cowboys
C) New York Giants
D) 49ers

6. **Which quarterback completed his first NFL pass to himself?**

A) Scott Tolzien
B) Matt Flynn
C) Jordan Love
D) Brett Favre

7. **What number did the Packers retire in honor of Don Hutson?**

A) 15
B) 3
C) 66
D) 14

8. **Which Packer has scored the most touchdowns?**

A) Jordy Nelson
B) Don Hutson
C) Jim Taylor
D) Davante Adams

9. **Who was the first Packers quarterback selected to the Pro Bowl since Bart Starr in 1966?**

A) Lynn Dickey
B) Don Majkowski
C) Brett Favre
D) Randy Wright

10. **Which player has been selected to the most Pro Bowls as a Packer?**

A) Brett Favre
B) Aaron Rodgers
C) Forrest Gregg
D) Willie Wood

CHAPTER 11 ANSWERS

1. (A) 1

Bart Starr won the NFL's Most Valuable Player (MVP) award only once, in 1966. Starr was also named MVP in Super Bowl I and II.

2. (D) Jordan Love

Jordan Love holds the record for the highest single-game playoff passer rating by a Packers quarterback, achieving a 157.2 passer rating against the Cowboys in Dallas in the Wildcard game on January 14, 2024. He had a perfect rating at one point but unfortunately threw one last incomplete pass in garbage time.

3. (C) Curly Lambeau

Curly Lambeau is the only player in Packers history to have worn number 1 on their jersey. Although this number is not officially retired by the team, no other player has worn it. He was a player, the team's co-founder, and their first head coach.

4. (B) Donald Driver

Donald Driver is the all-time leading receiver for the Packers, amassing 10,137 yards from 1999 to 2012. He's followed by James Lofton with 9,656 yards, Sterling Sharpe with 8,134, and Davante Adams with 8,121. In his 14 seasons, all with Green Bay, he made the Pro Bowl 4 times and won the Super Bowl in 2011.

5. (D) 49ers

Despite their first postseason matchup occurring as recently as 1996, the Packers have faced the 49ers in the playoffs more often than any other team. Including the 2024 divisional round loss at San Francisco, the Packers trail the 49ers in the series 4-6.

6. (D) Brett Favre

Against the Tampa Bay Buccaneers in 1992, Favre's first career NFL completion was a pass tipped back to himself, which he caught for a loss of 7 yards.

7. (D) 14

The Packers retired the number 14 in honor of Don Hutson, a testament to his groundbreaking impact on the team and the sport of football. Hutson, a receiver who revolutionized the passing game, set numerous NFL records during his career in the 1930s and 1940s.

8. (B) Don Hutson

Don Hutson leads the Packers with a record of 105 total touchdowns, a tally that includes 99 TD receptions, 3 rushing TDs, 1 interception returned for a TD, and 2 others from blocked kicks/missed field goals. Achieving this remarkable feat between 1935 and 1945, Hutson's scoring set him apart from other Packer touchdown leaders, with Jim Taylor at 91 touchdowns, Davante Adams at 73, and Jordy Nelson at 69.

9.   (B) Don Majkowski

It had been 23 years since the Packers had a Pro Bowl quarterback. In 1989, Don Majkowski led the Packers to a 10-6 record, their first season in 17 years to win more than 8 games. The Majik Man became known for his comeback victories with 5 that season, finishing the year with 27 touchdowns and leading the league with 4,318 passing yards. Majkowski was selected to the only Pro Bowl of his career and was MVP runner-up to Joe Montana.

10. (B) Aaron Rodgers

Aaron Rodgers has been selected to the Pro Bowl 10 times as a Packer, with selections in 2009, 2011, 2012, 2014, 2015, 2016, 2018, 2019, 2020, and 2021. Hall of Famers Forrest Gregg had 9, Brett Favre had 9, and Willie Wood had 8 Pro Bowl selections.

12

CHAPTER 12

1. **What was the nickname for the running back tandem of Jim Taylor & Paul Hornung?**

   A) Thunder and Lightning
   B) Smash and Dash
   C) Blood and Stone
   D) Fire and Ice

2. **Which team did the Packers play in Super Bowl XXXI (31)?**

   A) Oakland Raiders
   B) Kansas City Chiefs
   C) Pittsburgh Steelers
   D) New England Patriots

3. **How many NFL Championships did Curly Lambeau win?**

   A) 5
   B) 2
   C) 4
   D) 6

4. **Which team did Ron Wolf trade a first-round pick in exchange for Brett Favre?**

   A) Atlanta Falcons
   B) New Orleans Saints
   C) Seattle Seahawks
   D) Cleveland Browns

5. **What position did Forrest Gregg play in the NFL?**

A) Defensive End
B) Offensive Tackle
C) Linebacker
D) Wide Receiver

6. **Which player set an NFL record for scoring 176 points during the 1960 season?**

A) Jim Taylor
B) Paul Hornung
C) Bart Starr
D) Don Hutson

7. **In 1919, which company sponsored the Packers, paid for their uniforms and equipment, and gave the team their name?**

A) Indian Packing Company
B) Green Bay Canning Company
C) Wisconsin Meat Packers
D) Acme Packers

8. **Which Packer has the most rushing touchdowns?**

A) Verne Lewellen
B) Ahman Green
C) Jim Taylor
D) Paul Hornung

9. What position did Herb Adderley play?

A) Safety
B) Kicker
C) Cornerback
D) Wide Receiver

10. Who has the most rushing touchdowns in Packers playoffs?

A) Edgar Bennett
B) John Kuhn
C) Aaron Rodgers
D) Aaron Jones

CHAPTER 12 ANSWERS

1. (A) Thunder and Lightning

Fullback Jim Taylor was the power back portion of the tandem while Paul Hornung was the all-purpose halfback. Hornung, known as "The Golden Boy," provided the lightning with his speed and versatility, while Taylor brought the thunder, pounding defenses with grit and toughness. Together, they formed one of the most formidable backfields in NFL history, playing alternating roles in the Packers' dominance during the 1960s.

2. (D) New England Patriots

The Packers defeated the New England Patriots 35-21 in Super Bowl XXXI (31), their first title in 29 years. On the second play of the game, Brett Favre audibled to a play he had seen in his hotel room that Joe Montana executed in a previous Super Bowl, hitting Andre Rison for a 54-yard touchdown pass. Favre later threw an 81-yard pass to Antonio Freeman, but it was Desmond Howard, with his 99-yard kickoff return for a touchdown, who won the Super Bowl MVP award.

3. (D) 6

Curly Lambeau was the first NFL head coach to achieve a three-peat by winning 3 NFL Championships consecutively from 1929 to 1931. He won 3 more NFL Championships in 1936, 1939, and 1944. The only other head coach to three-peat was Vince Lombardi, winning 3 straight titles from 1965 to 1967. Besides the Packers, no other NFL team has ever won 3 championships in a row.

4.   (A) Atlanta Falcons

In 1992, Ron Wolf traded a first-round pick for Atlanta Falcons quarterback Brett Favre. This one move changed the trajectory of the Packers for decades, restoring a championship-winning tradition absent for 3 decades. As a Jets executive the year prior, Wolf had wanted to draft Favre but missed him by one pick. As the Packers new GM, one of Wolf's first actions was to rescue Favre, who was relegated to a third-string backup under Jerry Glanville.

5.   (B) Offensive Tackle

Hall of Famer Forrest Gregg played 15 seasons for the Packers as an offensive tackle, mostly at right tackle. He was selected as an All-Pro 8 straight years, from 1960 to 1967. He set a league record for playing in 188 consecutive games, earning him the nickname "Iron Man". He won 5 NFL Championships with the Packers and 1 with the Cowboys, making him one of four players to ever win 6+ NFL titles (Tom Brady, Herb Adderley, and Fuzzy Thurston being the other three).

6.   (B) Paul Hornung

Paul Hornung, as a halfback and a kicker, led the NFL in scoring three straight years, from 1959 to 1961. In 1960, he set the record for most points scored in a single season in NFL history. That record, established in a 12-game season, stood for 46 years despite the NFL later expanding to 14 and then 16-game seasons.

7. (A) Indian Packing Company

In 1919, while working as a shipping clerk for the Indian Packing Company, Curly Lambeau asked his boss, Frank Peck, for $500 to buy uniforms and equipment for a new professional football team he was starting. In exchange for this sponsorship, Lambeau named the team after his employer - the Indian Packers.

8. (C) Jim Taylor

Jim Taylor holds the record for the most rushing touchdowns by a Packer, with a total of 81. He's followed by Ahman Green with 54 rushing TDs, Paul Hornung with 50, and Aaron Jones with 45.

9. (C) Cornerback

Hall of Famer Herb Adderley, drafted #12 overall in the 1961 NFL draft, played cornerback for the Packers for 9 seasons. Originally a halfback, he moved to cornerback because the Packers already had Jim Taylor and Paul Hornung in the backfield. He is the first player with a Super Bowl pick-six, intercepting Daryle Lamonica in Super Bowl II, returning it 60 yards to the house. He is the first NFL player to surpass 1,000+ interception return yards. Along with Tom Brady, Forrest Gregg, and Fuzzy Thurston, he is one of four players to ever win six or more NFL titles.

10. (D) Aaron Jones

Aaron Jones holds the record for the most rushing touchdowns in Packers playoffs, with a total of 7. Edgar Bennett had 5 playoff rushing TDs, and John Kuhn, Aaron Rodgers, and Dorsey Levens all had 4.

CHAPTER 13

1. **Which Packer was inducted into the Pro Football Hall of Fame in 2022?**

    A) Jerry Kramer
    B) LeRoy Butler
    C) Bobby Dillon
    D) Charles Woodson

2. **How long was the longest touchdown reception in Packers history?**

    A) 99 yards
    B) 98 yards
    C) 101 yards
    D) 96 yards

3. **Which network held the rights to nationally televise AFL games at the time of Super Bowl I?**

    A) NBC
    B) ABC
    C) CBS
    D) PBS

4. **Who broke Sterling Sharpe's Packers record for career receptions?**

    A) Donald Driver
    B) Davante Adams
    C) Jordy Nelson
    D) Greg Jennings

5. **Which Packer quarterback has the most rushing touchdowns?**

A) Brett Favre
B) Tobin Rote
C) Aaron Rodgers
D) Bart Starr

6. **What number did the Packers retire in honor of Bart Starr?**

A) 5
B) 14
C) 3
D) 15

7. **Who was the head coach of the Packers during the 1991 season before being replaced by Mike Holmgren?**

A) Ray Rhodes
B) Mike Sherman
C) Forrest Gregg
D) Lindy Infante

8. **What was the original name of the new stadium built in Green Bay in 1957?**

A) Green Bay Field
B) Lambeau Field
C) City Stadium
D) County Stadium

9. **Who was the star player known as the "Babe Ruth of football" for the Packers?**

   A) Don Hutson
   B) Paul Hornung
   C) Curly Lambeau
   D) Bart Starr

10. **Which NFL team did Reggie White play for before he signed with the Packers?**

    A) Pittsburgh Steelers
    B) New York Giants
    C) Dallas Cowboys
    D) Philadelphia Eagles

CHAPTER 13 ANSWERS

1. (B) LeRoy Butler

Hall of Famer Leroy Butler played all 12 of his seasons at safety for the Packers, from 1990 to 2001, including a win in Super Bowl XXXI (31). Despite being confined to a wheelchair as a kid, Butler went on to invent the Lambeau Leap! After Reggie White recovered a fumble forced by Butler, White lateraled it back to Butler who took it in stride through the end zone and jumped into the stands, starting the best touchdown tradition in the NFL.

2. (A) 99 yards

It doesn't get any longer than 99 yards. In 1995 against the Bears, Brett Favre dropped back into his end zone and launched a bomb to Robert Brooks, who took it all the way down the field for the touchdown. This reception is one of just thirteen 99-yarders in NFL history.

3. (A) NBC

In 1967, NBC held the rights to nationally televise AFL games while CBS had the rights to NFL games. This made Super Bowl I the only Super Bowl to be simulcast by two networks. Unfortunately, both networks completely wiped their game tapes, as was common at the time. It took until the 2010s to recover complete footage of the game, including illegal copies stored in attics, NFL Films, and various other sources.

4. (A) Donald Driver

From living in a U-Haul as a teen, to being drafted by Green Bay in the 7th round, to setting the Packer records for career receptions and receiving yards, Donald Driver spent his 14 NFL seasons as an all-time fan favorite. Driver caught 743 receptions from 1999 to 2012, surpassing Sterling Sharpe's 595 in October 2009. Davante Adams also passed Sharpe, catching 669 in his time as a Packer.

5. (C) Aaron Rodgers

Aaron Rodgers rushed for the most touchdowns as a Packers quarterback with 35. Tobin Rote had 29 rushing TDs, Bart Starr had 15, and Brett Favre had 13.

6. (D) 15

The Packers retired the number 15 in honor of Bart Starr, commemorating his extraordinary contributions to the team as both a player and a coach. Starr's leadership and performance, particularly in clutch moments like the Ice Bowl, were instrumental in the Packers 5 NFL Championships, including victories in Super Bowls I and II.

7. (D) Lindy Infante

Lindy Infante coached the Packers for 4 years, from 1988 to 1991 and had a record of 24-40. His best season came in 1989 when he coached the team to a 10-6 record, their first winning record in years, and was named Coach of the Year. After 3 out of 4 losing seasons, Infante was replaced by Mike Holmgren in 1992.

8.   (C) City Stadium

In 1957, the Packers moved from the original City Stadium located behind Green Bay East High School to "New" City Stadium near Ashwaubenon, the first stadium purposely built for an NFL team. It cost $960,000 to build and could accommodate 32,132 fans. The Packers won their inaugural game on the new field, beating the Bears 21-17. After 8 seasons, the Packers renamed the stadium "Lambeau Field" in honor of the Packers founder, player, and first coach.

9.   (A) Don Hutson

Don Hutson's dominance in football is often compared to Babe Ruth's, Wayne Gretzky's, and Michael Jordan's. When Hutson retired in 1945, he held 18 different NFL records. He led the league in various offensive categories 33 times, which till this day is still 7 more than the next closest all-time great, Jim Brown. His NFL record of 99 touchdown receptions stood for 44 years. Hutson had 30 interceptions, 1 pick-six, and led the league in interceptions as a safety in 1940. As a kicker, he led the NFL in field goals one season and extra points in 3 seasons. In 1943, Hutson led the league in receptions, TD receptions, yards, yards per game, scrimmage yards per touch, field goals, interception yards, interceptions returned for a TD, and overall points.

10. (D) Philadelphia Eagles

Before signing with the Packers, Reggie White played 2 seasons for the USFL's Memphis Showboats and 8 seasons for the Philadelphia Eagles. When White left both the Eagles and the Packers, he left as each team's all-time sack leader. As a free agent in 1993, White announced he would sign wherever God sent him. In response, Mike Holmgren left a message on White's answering machine, "Reggie, this is God. Come to Green Bay." So, he did.

Don Hutson, Date Unknown

LEVEL III

Ultimate Die-Hard Packers Trivia

CHAPTER 14

1. **What was the game-time temperature at Lambeau Field for the 1967 "Ice Bowl"?**

   A) 0 °F
   B) -13 °F
   C) -15 °F
   D) -10 °F

2. **Since 1994, which Packer has the most solo and assisted tackles?**

   A) Nick Barnett
   B) A.J. Hawk
   C) Morgan Burnett
   D) LeRoy Butler

3. **Which Packer was known as "The Golden Boy"?**

   A) Bart Starr
   B) Jim Taylor
   C) Aaron Rodgers
   D) Paul Hornung

4. **How long was the longest punt by a Packer?**

   A) 95 yards
   B) 85 yards
   C) 100 yards
   D) 90 yards

5. Which Packer has scored the most 2-point conversions?

A) Greg Jennings
B) Jamaal Williams
C) Aaron Rodgers
D) Davante Adams

6. What high school did Arnie Herber attend?

A) Madison West High School
B) Racine Case High School
C) Burlington High School
D) Green Bay West High School

7. Which player was named MVP in 1966?

A) Willie Davis
B) Willie Wood
C) Bart Starr
D) Ray Nitschke

8. Which team did Green Bay defeat in its largest road game comeback?

A) Chicago Bears
B) Los Angeles Rams
C) New Orleans Saints
D) Dallas Cowboys

9. **In the controversial 1989 "Instant Replay Game" against the Bears, what penalty was overturned upon review?**

A) Illegal Forward Pass
B) Holding Infraction
C) Pass Interference
D) Offside Violation

10. **Which Packer holds the record for most receiving yards per game in a season?**

A) Jordy Nelson
B) Sterling Sharpe
C) Don Hutson
D) James Lofton

CHAPTER 14 ANSWERS

1. (C) -15 °F

The game-time temperature at Lambeau Field for the 1967 NFL Championship Game, known as the "Ice Bowl", was -15 °F, with an average wind chill of -36 °F. It was so cold that they had to sell the beer (Pabst Blue Ribbon) at room temperature from the restrooms to keep it from freezing.

2. (B) A.J. Hawk

A.J. Hawk had 922 tackles (629 solo, 293 assists). LeRoy Butler had the most solo tackles (720, with 169 assists). Nick Barnett had 789, and Morgan Burnett had 698.

3. (D) Paul Hornung

Paul Hornung, known as "The Golden Boy," was a versatile and dynamic player for the Packers during the 1960s. His exceptional abilities as a halfback, placekicker, and passer made him a key contributor to the Packers' success under coach Vince Lombardi.

4. (D) 90 yards

In 1965, Don Chandler booted a 90-yard punt from the 10-yard line into the 49ers end zone.

5. (D) Davante Adams

Davante Adams converted 4 two-point attempts from 2014 - 2021. Jennings, Rodgers, and Williams each converted 3.

6. (D) Green Bay West High School

Green Bay native Arnie Herber played high school basketball and football at Green Bay West and freshman football at UW Madison before flunking out and joining the Packers as a handyman. Given a tryout by Curly Lambeau, Herber went on to become one of the first great passers in NFL history. He led the league in passing 3 times, played on 4 NFL Championship teams, and set the record for career passing yards with 6,749 when he retired as a Packer. Herber joined the Giants in 1944 and faced Lambeau and the Packers in the NFL Championship Game, losing to Green Bay 14-7.

7. (C) Bart Starr

Bart Starr was awarded his one and only MVP in 1966. In that season, the Packers had 12 All-Pro players on the team that went on to win Super Bowl I.

8. (D) Dallas Cowboys

In their 2013 matchup at AT&T Stadium, Packers were down by 23 before Matt Flynn led a comeback to beat the Cowboys 37 - 36.

9. (A) Illegal Forward Pass

Don Majkowski's touchdown pass to Sterling Sharpe was originally called over the line. But upon a long-lasting instant replay review, the pass was deemed legal, which allowed the game-winning touchdown to stand.

10. (C) Don Hutson

Don Hutson had 1211 receiving yards in 11 games in 1942, for an average of 110.1 yards per game.

CHAPTER 15

1. **Who was the first African American to play in the regular season for the Packers?**

   A) Herb Adderley
   B) Dave Robinson
   C) Bob Mann
   D) Willie Davis

2. **Which Packer had the most kick returns and yards in a single season?**

   A) Roell Preston
   B) Dave Hampton
   C) Allen Rossum
   D) Will Blackmon

3. **What primary position did Jerry Kramer play?**

   A) Center
   B) Guard
   C) Offensive Tackle
   D) Tight End

4. **Which former Green Bay mayor served as the Packers president for 24 years?**

   A) Bob Harlan
   B) Russ Bogda
   C) Dominic Olejniczak
   D) Lee Joannes

5. **What was the name of the stadium the Packers moved to in 1925?**

A) City Stadium
B) Hagemeister Park
C) Bellevue Park
D) Borchert Field

6. **Which player was named the NFL MVP for the 1961 season?**

A) Willie Wood
B) Bart Starr
C) Paul Hornung
D) Jim Taylor

7. **Who holds the team record for most rushing touchdowns in a season?**

A) Aaron Jones
B) Jim Taylor
C) Ahman Green
D) Paul Hornung

8. **Which of these Packer kickers had the highest career field goal completion rate?**

A) Ryan Longwell
B) Jan Stenerud
C) Chris Jacke
D) Mason Crosby

9.   **Which Packer has caught the most interceptions?**

A) Charles Woodson
B) Willie Wood
C) Bobby Dillon
D) Herb Adderley

10. **How many interceptions did Herb Adderley record as a Packer?**

A) 37
B) 35
C) 39
D) 41

CHAPTER 15 ANSWERS

1.   (C) Bob Mann

Bob Mann joined the Packers in 1950 and is recognized as the first Black to break the color barrier in Green Bay. The following season, he led the Packers with 50 catches, 696 yards, & 8 TD receptions.

2.   (A) Roell Preston

In 1998, Roell Preston returned 57 kickoffs for 1,497 yards.

3.   (B) Guard

Hall of Famer, 5-time NFL Champion, and 5-time All-Pro Jerry Kramer played guard for the Packers for 11 seasons, from 1958 to 1968. He was a driving factor in the infamous Packers Sweep, which involved Kramer pulling from his guard position and lead-blocking for Jim Taylor and Paul Hornung to "run to daylight". It was Kramer's block that allowed Bart Starr to score the winning touchdown in the 1967 Ice Bowl against the Cowboys. Kramer doubled as a kicker, leading the NFL in field goal percentage in 1962, and he was the Packers' leading scorer with 91 points in 1963.

4.   (C) Dominic Olejniczak

Former Green Bay mayor, Dominic Olejniczak, was Packers president from 1958 to 1982. When he took over, the team had a losing record for 10 years. He's credited with a stock sale that kept the team afloat, hiring Lombardi, advocating for the new City Stadium, and shepherding the organization to 5 NFL Championships.

5. (A) City Stadium

The Packers were founded in 1919, two years before joining the NFL in 1921. George Calhoun, an editor at the Green Bay Press-Gazette, suggested to Earl "Curly" Lambeau, who had dropped out of Notre Dame football due to illness, that they should start a professional football team in Green Bay. Calhoun served as the team's publicist and manager, and Lambeau served as the team's coach, captain, and halfback.

6. (C) Paul Hornung

Paul Hornung was named Most Valuable Player for the 1961 season despite being temporarily called up to active duty as a reservist in the U.S. Army in response to the building of the Berlin Wall. He missed one game as a result but was able to get weekend passes to play other games.

7. (B) Jim Taylor

Jim Taylor set the Packers record by scoring 19 rushing touchdowns in 1962 and was named the NFL's MVP. Taylor rushed for 1,474 yards that year, making him the only player to ever out-rush Jim Brown in a season.

8. (A) Ryan Longwell

Among Packers kickers, Ryan Longwell holds the highest career field goal completion rate at 81.6%. His performance slightly edges out Mason Crosby's 81.4%, Jan Stenerud's 80.8%, and Chris Jacke's 77.2%.

9. (C) Bobby Dillon

Safety Bobby Dillon holds the record for the most interceptions caught by a Packer, with an impressive total of 52 interceptions from 1952 to 1959. Dillon's interception record stands today despite playing in an era when the passing game was not as prevalent as it is today.

10. (C) 39

Adderley had 39 interceptions as a Packer across 9 seasons. His 7 TDs returned for a touchdown was a record until Charles Woodson surpassed that mark. He still shares a record with Woodson and Nick Collins for 3 pick-sixes in a season.

16

CHAPTER 16

1. **Which stadium hosted Super Bowl II?**

   A) Los Angeles Memorial Coliseum
   B) Orange Bowl
   C) Rose Bowl
   D) Cotton Bowl

2. **Who did the Packers beat in the 1964 "Free Kick Game" where Paul Hornung made an extremely rare 52-yard "fair catch kick"?**

   A) Chicago Bears
   B) Baltimore Colts
   C) St. Louis Cardinals
   D) Cleveland Browns

3. **Which Packer has forced the most fumbles?**

   A) Kabeer Gbaja-Biamila
   B) Clay Matthews
   C) Reggie White
   D) Charles Woodson

4. **If Packers shareholders were to sell the team, where would the proceeds go?**

   A) Green Bay Packers Foundation
   B) American Legion
   C) City of Green Bay
   D) Current Shareholders

5. Which Packer tackle is the only person to be inducted into the Pro Football Hall of Fame and Baseball Hall of Fame?

A) Cal Hubbard
B) Bob Skoronski
C) Jerry Kramer
D) Forrest Gregg

6. Who was the head coach of the Packers in 1979?

A) Ray McLean
B) Gene Ronzani
C) Lisle Blackbourn
D) Hugh Devore

7. What was the final score of Super Bowl I?

A) 33 - 14 Packers
B) 35 - 10 Packers
C) 31 - 17 Packers
D) 21 - 17 Packers

8. Who was the head coach of the Packers in 1970?

A) Vince Lombardi
B) Dan Devine
C) Bart Starr
D) Phil Bengtson

9. **What position did Willie Davis play in the NFL?**

   A) Cornerback
   B) Linebacker
   C) Safety
   D) Defensive End

10. **Which college did All-American Paul Hornung attend?**

    A) Notre Dame
    B) Purdue
    C) Michigan
    D) Penn State

CHAPTER 16 ANSWERS

1.   (B) Orange Bowl

Super Bowl II was hosted at the Orange Bowl in Miami, Florida, on January 14, 1968. Miami, as an AFL city, was chosen to help establish credibility and balance between the two conferences. Also, attendance at the previous year's Super Bowl at the LA Coliseum was underwhelming, and the Orange Bowl had proven itself by hosting several previous Playoff Bowls.

2.   (A) Chicago Bears

There's an obscure NFL rule called the "fair catch free kick" rule that allows a team who fair catches a punt the option to place kick a field goal with the defense backed up 10 yards, like a kickoff, so the receiving team has a "free kick". In 1964, Elijah Pitts fair caught a punt on the 48-yard line in Green Bay territory. Lombardi called for the free kick, so Bart Starr held the ball while Paul Hornung made a 52-yard field goal. The Packers beat the Bears 23-12.

3.   (A) Kabeer Gbaja-Biamila

Kabeer Gbaja-Biamila (or KGB) holds the record for the most forced fumbles by a Packer, with a total of 17 from 2000 to 2008.

4. (A) Green Bay Packers Foundation

The Packers' bylaws state the proceeds of a sale would be given to the Packers Foundation to fund charitable causes. Before 1997, the original bylaws stated the proceeds would go to a local American Legion post to fund "a proper soldier's memorial".

5. (A) Cal Hubbard

Cal Hubbard, a former Packers tackle, holds the unique distinction of being the only individual inducted into both the Pro Football Hall of Fame and the Baseball Hall of Fame. Beyond his dual-sport legacy, Hubbard is also a member of the College Hall of Fame and is credited as one of the inventors of the linebacker position. His innovative approach to playing off the 7-man line laid the groundwork for the modern-day linebacker role.

6. (B) Gene Ronzani

After 31 years as the Packers' first and only head coach, Curly Lambeau gave way to Gene Ronzani in 1950. Ronzani lasted only 4 seasons, posting one of the worst records in Packers history, going 14-31-1. Ronzani resigned mid-season 1953 after a brutal loss on national TV to Detroit on Thanksgiving Day.

7. (B) 35 - 10 Packers

The Packers beat the Chiefs in the first-ever Super Bowl 35-10. Bart Starr threw 2 touchdowns to Max McGee, Elijah Pitts had 2 rushing touchdowns, and Jim Taylor scored on a 14-yard run. Don Chandler kicked 5 extra points.

8. (D) Phil Bengtson

Phil Bengtson won 5 NFL Championships as defensive coordinator for the Packers from 1959 to 1967 and succeeded Vince Lombardi as head coach in 1968. With players aging out, Bengston's Packers could only muster a 20-21-1 record over 3 seasons, so Bengston was let go after the 1970 season.

9. (D) Defensive End

Hall of Famer, 5-time NFL Champion, and 6-time All-Pro Willie Davis played defensive end for the Packers for 10 seasons. He is the unofficial all-time sack leader for the Packers. Sack statistics were not officially kept during his time, but he is known to have at least 100 sacks, possibly 120 or more, including 25 in one season alone. Davis was drafted in the 15th round in 1956, served in the U.S. Army for 2 years, and played for the Cleveland Browns before being traded to the Pack in 1960.

10. (A) Notre Dame

Paul Hornung, a Heisman Trophy winner and All-American at Notre Dame, was the first overall pick in the 1957 NFL draft. Hornung is one of nine NFL MVPs to also have won the Heisman.

CHAPTER 17

1. **What was the final score of the Ice Bowl between the Packers and the Cowboys?**

   A) Packers 24, Cowboys 21
   B) Packers 21, Cowboys 17
   C) Cowboys 21, Packers 17
   D) Packers 17, Cowboys 14

2. **Which Packer has made the most QB hits since 2006?**

   A) Aaron Kampman
   B) Rashan Gary
   C) Preston Smith
   D) Clay Matthews

3. **How many former Packers have been inducted into the Pro Football Hall of Fame?**

   A) 34
   B) 31
   C) 29
   D) 33

4. **Prior to becoming General Manager, what position did Brian Gutekunst hold with the Packers?**

   A) Director of College Scouting
   B) Senior Personnel Executive
   C) Director of Player Personnel
   D) Director of Football Operations

5. **Which Kenosha native was Executive Vice President of Football Operations and drafted Sterling Sharpe, LeRoy Butler, & Tony Mandarich?**

A) Bob Harlan
B) Ron Wolf
C) Tom Braatz
D) Ted Thompson

6. **What was the final score of Super Bowl II?**

A) 24 - 17 Packers
B) 35 - 10 Packers
C) 21 - 17 Packers
D) 33 - 14 Packers

7. **Who was the first NFL player to pass for 2,000 yards or more?**

A) Cecil Isbell
B) Tobin Rote
C) Jack Jacobs
D) Arnie Herber

8. **What are the most touchdowns Brett Favre has thrown in a season?**

A) 41
B) 38
C) 39
D) 40

9. **Which team outside the NFL North has the Packers played the most?**

A) San Francisco 49ers
B) Tampa Bay Buccaneers
C) Los Angeles Rams
D) Arizona Cardinals

10. **What position did Carroll Dale play in the NFL?**

A) Linebacker
B) Tight end
C) Wide receiver
D) Running back

CHAPTER 17 ANSWERS

1.   (B) Packers 21, Cowboys 17

The Packers trailed the Cowboys 14 - 17 with less than 5 minutes remaining. Starting from their 32-yard line, facing -50 °F wind chills, they drove to the Cowboy's 1 yard line. After two failed run attempts and seconds left on the board, Lombardi & Starr decided on a QB sneak. Starr called a fullback wedge in the huddle, but never told his teammates he intended to keep it and run it himself. Following Jerry Kramer and Ken Bowman's double-team, Starr lunged in to take the lead, for a final score of 21 - 17.

2.   (D) Clay Matthews

Since 2006, when they started tracking this stat, Clay Matthews has recorded the most quarterback hits for the Packers, with a total of 189. Other top Packers include Aaron Kampman with 100 QB hits, Preston Smith with 92, Rashan Gary with 76, and Kenny Clark with 71.

3.   (D) 33

33 former Packers are in the Pro Football Hall of Fame. 28 members who spent a major portion of their career as a Packer have their names on the ring of honor at Lambeau Field, the most recent being LeRoy Butler in 2022.

4. (C) Director of Player Personnel

Before ascending to the role of general manager for the Packers, Brian Gutekunst served as the Director of Player Personnel. In this capacity, Gutekunst was instrumental in scouting and evaluating talent, contributing significantly to the team's drafting strategy and roster construction. His expertise in identifying and developing players was a key factor in his promotion to general manager.

5. (C) Tom Braatz

Tom Braatz, a Kenosha native, served as the Executive Vice President of Football Operations for the Packers, where he played a pivotal role in drafting notable players such as Sterling Sharpe, LeRoy Butler, and Tony Mandarich.

6. (D) 33 - 14 Packers

The Packers beat the Raiders in the second Super Bowl, with Don Chandler kicking 4 field goals and 3 extra points, Boyd Dowler scoring on a 62-yard touchdown catch, Donny Anderson running in a touchdown, and Herb Adderley returning an interception 60 yards into the end zone.

7. (A) Cecil Isbell

Cecil Isbell broke new ground in the NFL by becoming the first player to pass for over 2,000 yards in a season, recording a total of 2,021 yards in 1942.

8. (C) 39

In 1996, Brett Favre achieved a personal best by throwing 39 touchdowns during the regular season. Favre went on to win Super Bowl XXXI (31) that season.

9. (C) Los Angeles Rams

The Packers have met the Rams 99 times (as of 2023), leading the matchup 50 - 47 - 2, including a 2 - 1 postseason record. The Pack have played the Cardinals 75 times, 49ers 63 times, and the Buccaneers 57 times.

10. (C) Wide receiver

Carroll Dale played 8 seasons at wide receiver for the Packers from 1965 to 1972, winning three straight NFL Championships. Known for his big play, deep threat ability, Dale had a 47-yard catch in the 1965 NFL title game, a 51-yard touchdown in the 1966 NFL title game and set the Packers franchise record for yards per catch with 19.7.

18

CHAPTER 18

1. **Who was the head coach of the Packers during the 2000 season?**

   A) Mike McCarthy
   B) Mike Sherman
   C) Ray Rhodes
   D) Mike Holmgren

2. **Where did Brian Gutekunst attend college?**

   A) University of Wisconsin La Crosse
   B) Marquette University
   C) Ripon College
   D) University of Wisconsin Madison

3. **Who won the NFL Championship game in 1960?**

   A) New York Giants
   B) Green Bay Packers
   C) Philadelphia Eagles
   D) Detroit Lions

4. **What position did Dave Robinson play in the NFL?**

   A) Safety
   B) Defensive end
   C) Cornerback
   D) Linebacker

5. **Who led the NFL in interceptions during the 1962 season?**

A) Dan Currie
B) Hank Gremminger
C) Herb Adderley
D) Willie Wood

6. **What is the maximum number of stock shares that one individual is allowed to hold in the Packers?**

A) 150,000 shares
B) 250,000 shares
C) 300,000 shares
D) 200,000 shares

7. **Who was the head coach of the Packers in 1972?**

A) Ray McLean
B) Phil Bengtson
C) Dan Devine
D) Bart Starr

8. **What position did Henry Jordan play in the NFL?**

A) Linebacker
B) Cornerback
C) Safety
D) Defensive Tackle

9. **Who was the general manager of the Packers during the 1966 season?**

   A) Vince Lombardi
   B) Dominic Olejniczak
   C) No General Manager
   D) Phil Bengtson

10. **What was the brand name of the canned meat sold by the Indian Packing Company?**

    A) Council Meats
    B) Green Bay's Finest Meats
    C) Heritage Deli Meats
    D) Fox River Foods

CHAPTER 18 ANSWERS

1.   (B) Mike Sherman

Mike Sherman was head coach of the Packers from 2000 to 2005 and additionally served as General Manager from 2001 to 2004. Sherman had 5 straight winning seasons but never made it past the divisional round of the playoffs. After going 4-12 in 2005, their first losing season since 1991, Sherman was fired as head coach with an overall record of 57-39.

2.   (A) University of Wisconsin La Crosse

Brian Gutekunst played college football for the UW La Crosse Eagles as a defensive back before a shoulder injury permanently sidelined him. He stayed on the team as a student assistant, coaching the linebackers during their 1995 Division III National Championship season. Gutekunst joined the Packers as an intern in 1997 and eventually was promoted to General Manager in 2018.

3.   (C) Philadelphia Eagles

The Philadelphia Eagles emerged victorious in the NFL Championship game in 1960, defeating the Packers. This was Philadelphia's last championship win until their Super Bowl victory in 2018. It also stands as the only playoff defeat for Packers coach Vince Lombardi, who went on to win 5 of the next 7 NFL titles from 1961 to 1967.

4.   (D) Linebacker

Hall of Famer Dave Robinson was drafted by 3 teams: the Green Bay Packers, San Diego Chargers, and the Montreal Alouettes. The Chargers traded his rights to the Bills, and because Robinson's fiancé knew how cold it was in Buffalo, they chose Green Bay. Robinson played linebacker from 1963 to 1972, most notably alongside Ray Nitschke and Lee Roy Caffey, forming one of the best linebacker trios of all time. Robinson was a 3-time All-Pro and a 3-time NFL Champion. In the offseason, Robinson worked at Schlitz Brewery in Milwaukee, which eventually led to his second career in the beer business.

5.   (D) Willie Wood

Hall of Famer and 5-time NFL Champion Willie Wood was undrafted out of college as a quarterback, but he wrote Vince Lombardi a letter asking for a tryout. Signed as a free agent, Wood switched sides to defense and became a 9-time All-Pro safety. In 1962, Wood led the league in punt return yards and interceptions with 9 picks. In Super Bowl I, he intercepted Len Dawson for a 50-yard return. Wood finished his career with 48 interceptions.

6.   (D) 200,000 shares

In the unique ownership structure of Green Bay Packers, Inc., no one is allowed to hold more than 200,000 shares. This rule is part of the team's effort to prevent any single person from gaining control, ensuring the Packers remain a community-owned franchise. There are over 5,000,000 shares issued to over 500,000 shareholders.

7. (C) Dan Devine

Dan Devine lasted 4 seasons as the head coach of the Packers. From 1971 to 1974, the Packers were 25-27-1. Devine's one winning season came in 1972 when they went 10-4 and advanced to the playoffs. This was the Packers last playoff appearance in a non-strike year until 1993.

8. (D) Defensive Tackle

Hall of Fame defensive tackle Henry Jordan was traded from Cleveland to the Packers in 1959 for a fourth-round draft pick. With the Packers, he played in 6 NFL title games, winning 5 of them, and was named All-Pro 7 times. After he retired in 1969, he became the Executive Director of Summerfest in Milwaukee.

9. (A) Vince Lombardi

Vince Lombardi, serving as both the head coach and general manager for the Packers during the 1966 season, led the team to victory in Super Bowl I. Until 1981, it was typical for Packers' head coaches to also serve as the general manager.

10. (A) Council Meats

The Indian Packing Company packed meat into cans. "A meat market on your pantry shelf" was the slogan for their flagship brand, Council Meats. A few of their top sellers included Ol' Mammy Hash, Lunch Tongue, Veal Loaf, Vienna Style Sausage, Hamburger Steak and Onions, Potted Meat-Products, Tripe, Sliced Dried Beef, Sausage Meat, and Ox Tongue.

CHAPTER 19

1. **Who has kicked the most punts for the Packers?**

    A) Tim Masthay
    B) Don Bracken
    C) David Beverly
    D) Donny Anderson

2. **What is the seating capacity of Lambeau Field?**

    A) 83,597
    B) 79,735
    C) 85,459
    D) 81,441

3. **Who was the first NFL player to throw for more than 1,000 yards?**

    A) Cecil Isbell
    B) Tony Canadeo
    C) Arnie Herber
    D) Bob Monnett

4. **What primary position did Mike Michalske play for the Packers?**

    A) Tight End
    B) Guard
    C) Center
    D) Linebacker

5. **What was the final score of Super Bowl XXXI (31)?**

   A) 33 - 30 Packers
   B) 31 - 25 Packers
   C) 21 - 17 Packers
   D) 35 - 21 Packers

6. **Which Packer made the most tackles for a loss since 1999?**

   A) A.J. Hawk
   B) Kabeer Gbaja-Biamila
   C) Aaron Kampman
   D) Clay Matthews

7. **Who is the all-time leading punt returner for the Packers?**

   A) Phil Epps
   B) Willie Wood
   C) Antonio Chatman
   D) Al Carmichael

8. **Who was the president and CEO of the Packers before Mark Murphy?**

   A) Mike Sherman
   B) Ron Wolf
   C) Ted Thompson
   D) Bob Harlan

9. **What primary position did Johnny McNally play?**

A) Safety
B) Linebacker
C) Cornerback
D) Halfback

10. **Who is the all-time leading kick returner for the Packers?**

A) Al Carmichael
B) Herb Adderley
C) Steve Odom
D) Dave Hampton

CHAPTER 19 ANSWERS

1. (C) David Beverly

David Beverly is the prolific punter in Packers history with 495 punts in 86 games from 1975 to 1980.

2. (D) 81,441

Lambeau Field seats 81,441 fans, giving it the second highest capacity in the NFL behind MetLife Stadium's 82,500 seats. Debuting in 1957, the original stadium opened at full capacity with 32,132 fans and has since undergone 18 expansions. Since 1960, Lambeau Field has sold out every single game. The waitlist for season tickets is over 150,000 long. With an average of 300 getting access to season tickets per year, joining the waitlist now is an approximately 500-year wait.

3. (C) Arnie Herber

The NFL began keeping statistics in 1932, and in that year, Arnie Herber led the league in passing yards with 639. He led the league again in 1934 and 1936, becoming the first passer to ever throw for more than 1,000 yards, achieving a total of 1,239 in 1936. He retired from the Packers as the NFL's all-time leading passer with 6,749 yards.

4.   (B) Guard

Mike Michalske played guard for the Packers starting in 1929 and has been regarded as one of the best guards, maybe the best player overall, of the 1920s and 30s. Nicknamed "Iron Mike" because he often played the full 60 minutes of each game and only missed a few games in his 8 seasons as a Packer. He won 3 NFL Championships from 1929 to 1931 and was the first guard inducted into the Hall of Fame.

5.   (D) 35 - 21 Packers

The Packers beat the Patriots 35-21 at the Louisiana Superdome on January 26, 1997. Brett Favre threw a 54-yard bomb to Andre Rison to open the scoring. Favre had an even longer touchdown pass to Antonio Freeman, an 81-yarder. Chris Jacke kicked 2 field goals and 3 extra points. Favre scored again on a 2-yard keeper into the end zone. Finally, Desmond Howard returned a kickoff 99 yards for the final touchdown of the game, with Mark Chmura catching a 2-point conversion to end the day.

6.   (D) Clay Matthews

Since 1999, when they began tracking this stat, Clay Matthews leads the Packers with 121 tackles for a loss. Kabeer Gbaja-Biamila had 74, Aaron Kampan had 61, and A.J. Hawk had 55.

7. (B) Willie Wood

Willie Wood stands as the all-time leading punt returner for the Packers, amassing 187 returns for 1,391 yards and 2 touchdowns from 1960 to 1971. Wood's exceptional vision and agility made him a formidable threat in the return game, complementing his stellar defensive play as a safety.

8. (D) Bob Harlan

Bob Harlan began his role as President and CEO of the Packers in 1989 before Mark Murphy took over in 2008. Harlan revolutionized the decision-making structure by eliminating the Executive Committee from making football decisions and instead brought in future Hall of Famer Ron Wolf as General Manager with full control. Harlan is credited with the resurgence of the Packers that began in the 1990s, with Super Bowl wins under Wolf and Ted Thompson, another GM Harlan hired.

9. (D) Halfback

Before joining the Packers in 1925 as a halfback, Johnny "Blood" McNally played for the Milwaukee Badgers, Duluth Eskimos, and Pottsville Maroons. As a multiple-threat runner, passer, receiver, punter, and defender, Blood was the main playmaker other teams feared. Blood won 4 NFL titles with the Packers, played for 5 teams across 14 seasons, and was selected to the first-ever Hall of Fame class in 1963.

10. (C) Steve Odom

Steve Odom is the all-time leading kick returner for the Packers, with 179 returns for 4,124 yards and 2 touchdowns from 1974 to 1979.

20

CHAPTER 20

1. **Which Packer holds the record for most passes defended since 1999?**

    A) Tramon Williams
    B) Al Harris
    C) Charles Woodson
    D) Jaire Alexander

2. **What was the final score of Super Bowl XLV (45)?**

    A) 31 - 25 Packers
    B) 27 - 23 Packers
    C) 35 - 21 Packers
    D) 34 - 31 Packers

3. **Who's single-season record did Aaron Rodgers surpass when he threw for 4,643 yards in the 2011 season?**

    A) Lynn Dickey
    B) Bart Starr
    C) Brett Favre
    D) Don Majkowski

4. **Which player has been named as first-team All-Pro as a Packer the most often?**

    A) Don Hutson
    B) Lavvie Dilweg
    C) Forrest Gregg
    D) Jim Ringo

5. What position did Curly Lambeau play for the Packers?

A) Wide Receiver
B) Quarterback
C) Kicker
D) Halfback

6. Who has returned the most kickoffs for touchdowns as a Packer?

A) Al Carmichael
B) Travis Williams
C) Dave Hampton
D) Steve Odom

7. What was the name of the movie that aired in 1973, starring Ernest Borgnine as Vince Lombardi?

A) Legend in Granite
B) Dawn of a Dynasty
C) Leadership on the Line
D) Love and Legacy

8. Who was the head coach of the Packers in 1979?

A) Forrest Gregg
B) Dan Devine
C) Lindy Infante
D) Bart Starr

9. **What was the Packers' record in the 1989 season?**

    A) 8 - 8
    B) 10 - 6
    C) 1 - 15
    D) 2 - 14

10. **Which Packer was known as "The Gravedigger"?**

    A) Gilbert Brown
    B) Ryan Pickett
    C) B.J. Raji
    D) Johnny Jolly

CHAPTER 20 ANSWERS

1. (A) Tramon Williams

Cornerback Tramon Williams defended 125 passes from 2007 to 2019. Charles Woodson is second with 99 passes defended, followed by Al Harris with 87.

2. (A) 31 - 25 Packers

The Packers beat the Steelers 31-25 in Super Bowl XLV (45) at AT&T Stadium on February 6, 2011. The scoring began with a 29-yard touchdown catch by Jordy Nelson. Nick Collins intercepted Ben Roethlisberger and weaved his way through the defense and into the end zone. Greg Jennings caught two touchdowns from Aaron Rodgers, and Mason Crosby finished the day with a field goal and 4 extra points.

3. (A) Lynn Dickey

When Aaron Rodgers threw for 4,643 yards in a single season, he surpassed Lynn Dickey's record of 4,458 yards set in 1983. Dickey was the first NFC quarterback to pass for 4000+ yards, and his record stood for 28 years before Rodgers finally broke it with a historically great offense in 2011.

4. (A) Don Hutson

Don Hutson was named as a first-team All-Pro in an impressive 8 consecutive seasons from 1938 to 1945. Only Jerry Rice and Jim Otto with 10 and Ron Mix and Anthony Munoz with 9 have more first-team All-Pro selections.

5. (D) Halfback

Curly Lambeau not only co-founded the Packers and served as their first head coach for 31 years, but he also played halfback, making him the main passer and runner for 10 seasons. Lambeau scored 35 touchdowns in his playing career: 24 passing, 8 rushing, and 3 receiving. He also kicked a few field goals and extra points, making him the first player to throw a pass, throw a touchdown, and kick a field goal in Packers history.

6. (B) Travis Williams

Travis Williams holds the record for the most kickoffs returned for touchdowns as a Packer, with a total of 5 in just 4 seasons from 1967 to 1970. He still holds the NFL's single-season records set in 1967 for touchdown returns with 4 and kickoff return average with 41 yards per return. Known as "The Roadrunner", Williams was the first Packer to achieve 300+ yards in a game with 314 in a 1969 game against the Steelers where he returned both a kickoff and a punt for touchdowns, also a first for the Packers.

7. (A) Legend in Granite

The 1973 made-for-TV movie, "Legend in Granite", starred Ernest Borgnine portraying Vince Lombardi in his first 2 years as the coach of the Packers. Lombardi was one of the "Seven Blocks of Granite" offensive linemen at Fordham University in the 1930's. When he took over the Packers in 1959, the franchise hadn't had a winning season in over a decade. By 1960, the Packers reached the NFL Championship game but lost to the Philadelphia Eagles.

8. (D) Bart Starr

Bart Starr was head coach for 9 seasons, from 1975 to 1983. He was the third of five straight Packer head coaches with a losing record, going 52-76-3. Starr's best season was in the strike-shortened season of 1982 where his team went 5-3-1, made it to the playoffs for the first time in 10 years, and beat the St. Louis Cardinals in the first playoff game at Lambeau since 1967.

9. (B) 10 - 6

1989 was a magical year for the Packers, with Don "The Majik Man" Majkowski leading the team to a 10-6 record, their first non-strike winning season since 1972. The "Cardiac Pack" won 5 fourth-quarter comebacks and an NFL record 4 one-point wins.

10. (A) Gilbert Brown

Big Gilbert Brown, weighing upwards of 355 pounds, was known as the "Gravedigger" for his sack celebration where he air-dug graves for his opponents. Brown played 10 seasons for the Packers, winning the Super Bowl in 1996, and was inducted into the Green Bay Hall of Fame in 2008.

CREDITS

This book took an incredible amount of research and fact-checking to compile. I couldn't have done it without referencing a few publications. Please join me in thanking a few of those resources:

packers.com

pro-football-reference.com

wikipedia.org

statmuse.com

footballdb.com

profootballhof.com

CALL TO ACTION

If you enjoyed this book, please help others find it by telling your friends and family, or by leaving a rating on Amazon. It only takes a minute, and your recommendation can make a huge impact.

You can quickly reach the book page at:

joefletcher.net

Thank you!